The Perils of

HEAVY
THINKING

A Collection of Humorous Shorts

First Edition Printed and bound in USA
ISBN: 978-1-940222-39-4

Cover design by Kelsey Rice
Cover Photography by Victoria Sparkman
Interior by Kelsey Rice

In memory of Mr. Terry Thomas, my 10th grade English teacher. The only human being on the face of the earth who could get excited enough about Moby Dick to leap on a desk and scream, "Thar she blows!"

And to all the elementary school teachers who read aloud to their students, instilling the wonder and joy of books.

To a teacher
my hero

Writing can be fun

best wishes

Russell

Special Author's Edition

They say you are what you eat. The same holds true for your brain. From an early age, I fed mine a steady diet of Rocky & Bullwinkle, Looney Toons, and that thrilling Test Pattern that appeared on the screen when TV stations logged off the air.

People like Paul Henning and Sherwood Schwartz served up heaping helpings of delicacies such as *The Beverly Hillbillies*, *Green Acres*, and *Gilligan's Island*. For decades, I gorged on the humor of Groucho Marx, Mel Brooks, Jackie Gleason, and dozens of others without realizing the long-term effects and mental health hazards associated with that type of programming. Back in those days people like Jonathan Winters came without warning labels. How was I to know they'd leave a lasting impression on my feeble young mind?

Then one day, I opened the back cover of *Field & Stream* magazine and read a short piece written by some fellow named Patrick F. McManus. Two or three sentences into the article I came to the conclusion that this guy, McManus, suffered from a rare mental disorder that enabled him to turn mundane, everyday occurrences into a series of hilarious misadventures. I had an epiphany, right then and there, without even knowing what one was.

Since that fateful day, I've spent a great deal of time collecting irrational thoughts and absurd ideas, waiting for just the right moment to spring them on an unsuspecting public. Well, my friends, that day has finally come. Welcome to my amusement park. Before we take off, make sure you're securely strapped in and keep your hands and feet inside the ride at all times.

Russell Gayer, April 2014

The Perils of
HEAVY
THINKING
A Collection of Humorous Shorts

by Russell Gayer

P

Pen-L Publishing
Fayetteville, AR
Pen-L.com

CONTENTS

Important Stuff You Should Know

Dragonslayer 3

What to Wear? What to Wear?........................... 8

Dreams of Mediocrity 11

The Incident...16

Are You Healthy Enough to Go to the Hospital?...........24

The Path of Most Resistance.................................32

Donut Abuse...36

Courting the Fat Vote.......................................43

Classic –the "New" Old....................................46

The Ultimate Instructional Guide–How to Write

"How-to" Books 49

Intellectual Futility...56

Irritable Vowel Syndrome.................................62

Young Dr. Jung or Samurai Vasectomy 66

Outdoor Misadventures

Lost at Peter Bottom...75

The One That Got Away.....................................79

Sack of Suckers...84

The Carp Tournament.......................................90

Redneck GPS...94

More Than One Way to Skin a Skunk..........................100

Manufactured Tales

The Peterinarian...109

Heavy Thinking..114

Much Nothing About Ado 119

Life with Mona...123

Stolen Goods..126

The Dave Barry Experience.............................129

Mallard P.I. 131

Deadeye Dick & the Stranger from Coyote Gulch 134

Triple F..143

Meet Rachel Crofton

Peeves I Like to Pet...167

Raising Cain..170

The Food Triangle..217

Dodging Miss Daisy...220

Acknowledgements..223

About the Author...224

Important Stuff
You Should Know

The following documents contain top secret information which has been withheld from the general public. Even Homeland Security, the TSA, the IRS, are unaware of the content of these manuscripts. Due to the Freedom of Information Act, and at the urging of my publisher, I'm releasing these never-before-seen documents for the enlightenment of mankind. So, if you're fortunate enough to be reading this right now – consider yourself in an elite crowd.

Dragonslayer

There was a time when dragons roamed the hills and hollows of Northwest Arkansas. These monstrous beasts slithered around narrow back-roads, forded swollen streams, and roared down one-lane blacktops in search of prey, paralyzing their victims with ominous yellow flashing lights. Only the most courageous, naïve, or ill-prepared youngsters dared challenge such hideous monsters.

Naturally, my mother was eager to sign me up at the earliest age possible.

To promote my God-given talent as a natural for the job, she bragged to the school principal how I had single-handedly destroyed two tricycles and a Western Flyer red wagon. The man was obviously impressed, but adamant that all enlistees be six years old to enroll in the dragonslayer program. Alas, I was forced to sit-out another year.

Finally...the big day came. We stood by the mailbox and waited.

Armed with an oversized three-ring binder and a four-pack of number two pencils, I prepared to do battle with the dragon. Mom insisted I wear my finest armor for the occasion, the outfit she affectionately referred to as my "new school clothes."

Off in the distance, we could hear the monster approaching. Twelve months of anticipation faded in the early morning fog. Anxiety took up residence in my stomach. It twisted my organs into knots and gnawed at the very core of my being. I clutched the binder close to my chest and squeezed Mama's hand. The day of reckoning had come.

Forty feet long and mean as a scorned woman, it came charging toward us. Skidding to a halt within mere inches of my trembling body, it threw open its gigantic mouth and bathed us in carbon monoxide.

"This is Russell," said Mom, wiping the dust from her eyes. "He's going to be getting on here from now on. Make *sure* he's home in time for chores."

"Yes, Ma'am," said the voice at the top of the dragon's staircase-tongue. "Hop aboard, young man. We've got plenty of good seats."

Cautiously, I climbed the steps and heard the monster's teeth slam shut behind me. It had already consumed eight or ten kids, none of whom I'd ever met. I plopped down in the first row, unaware of the terror I was about to behold. Time after time, the beast stopped to gorge on unsuspecting youth until it could hold no more. Once full, it made a mad dash to a large cinder block building on the east side of Fayetteville.

We had barely arrived at Root Elementary School when the dragon became violently ill and began throwing up in front of a large double door. After expelling about one third of us, me included, it slammed its mouth shut and roared out of sight.

A couple of ill-tempered adults barked orders and herded us into the building. It was utter chaos. People were screaming, crying, and hollering for their mamas, and that was just the faculty and staff. All the children knew where to go and what to do – except me.

I wandered about like a zombie looking for an apocalypse. From out of nowhere, a little blonde-haired girl grabbed me by the arm.

"You look lost. What grade are you in?"

"I'm starting first," I said, in a weak tremble.

"Then you need to go to this table," she said, dragging me across the auditorium. On the way, she informed me her name was Shawn and that she was accustomed to helping 'little' kids. I gave no argument. After all, she was in the second grade.

After a lengthy enrollment where I was forced to repeat my name, address, and next of kin fourteen times, I was escorted down a long hallway to the last room on the left. My guide introduced me to the teacher who would be responsible for pounding knowledge into my pea-sized brain.

Mrs. Sticklebottom was a petite, homely woman with a no-nonsense attitude. After inspecting my binder, notebook paper, and number two yellow pencils, she informed me that I did *not* have the proper supplies for first grade.

In those days, parents had no Walmart to run to, so the school operated a supply store on the premises. This is where I received my first academic lesson involving logic and the human anatomy.

The size of one's fingers and hands is inversely proportioned to the size of the required writing utensil. For example, if you have fists like King Kong, your pencil should be no thicker than a toothpick. On the other hand, if you have fingers like Tinker Bell, you are forced to use crayons the size of a baseball bat. How they expected you to color within the lines when you couldn't see the paper for the crayon was beyond me.

The writing pads issued to first graders featured a series of bold and dashed lines. The lines resembled oversized music staffs. There were only three staffs per page, assuring the supply store of repeat customers. The lines were spread far enough apart that even legally blind teachers could review homework without eye strain.

The most important supply was a twelve-inch wooden ruler. I soon discovered this teaching instrument was not used for measuring, but to administer corporal punishment to those who broke the silence during nap time.

Upon being fully equipped with the tools of the trade, I was returned to my cell block.

A lady wearing an apron stopped by twice that day with trays of small milk cartons. She demanded we all cough up two cents apiece for cow juice. This was my second academic lesson – economics. You can make more money milking students than you can milking cows. Maybe there was something to this education stuff after all.

Late in the afternoon, a bell sounded, and the cell door yawned like a bear awakening from a long winter's nap. I dashed out the opening with the rest of the herd, thundering down the hall toward the cafeteria. Several parole officers corralled us in the courtyard and escorted us to the dragon feeding grounds. The yellow monsters were lined up nose to tail, smoking and belching fumes that burned my throat and eyes.

"What's your bus number?" asked the kid next to me.

"Number?" I froze like a pillar of salt. *Dragons had numbers?*

"Your bus number," he said, pointing to the big black digits near the dragon's mouth.

"I don't know. This is my first day."

"Well, you better find out." He flashed a grin. "I gotta go. Good luck."

I scanned the lines forming in front of each dragon's mouth, hoping to recognize at least one poor soul who had shared my morning ride in the belly of the beast. There was Shawn, waving her arms and beckoning me to climb aboard number thirteen. Swatting superstition and two black cats aside, I bounced up the stairs and found an empty seat near the front.

There was a constant roar inside the dragon as we caromed down the highway. The poor beast soon developed indigestion again and began spitting us out at irregular intervals. I crouched behind a seat and waited patiently for a chance to escape. An eternity later, the dragon charged down the hill toward my mailbox and home. Racing to the front, I grabbed the dragon by the throat, forced its mouth open, and leaped to safety.

I marched up the driveway, threw open the front door and stomped into the living room like a victorious knight returning from a crusade.

"Take off your school clothes," said Mom. "It's time to do chores."

I hung my head and sighed.

What, no pie?

Dragonslayers just don't get the respect they deserve.

What to wear?
What to wear?

I was in the clothing department of a sporting goods store recently and noticed an immense supply of Starter® brand athletic wear. A little star is embedded in the logo which would imply that the wearer is not only first-string, but capable of athletic prowess above and beyond the average competitor.

Having participated in sports in my younger days, I am keenly aware that only a small percentage of players get to be starters. Even fewer go on to become stars.

At the peak of my athletic ability, I was mediocre at best. The coach soon realized that I had a God-given talent for "getting in the way." This was no surprise since my Dad often remarked that I was "always in the way" when he tried to work in the garage. Coach thought he could take advantage of my "special gift" by putting me on the offensive line. This worked pretty well in practice against the defensive linemen on our team, who were of average size and not particularly fast.

When the season opener rolled around, I couldn't wait to get on the field and show my friends and family how I could use "getting in the way" to help our team win. The coach gave a rousing pep-talk in the dressing room and I could feel adrenaline pumping through every vein. We ran screaming through the paper banner under the goal post while the marching band played our fight song, *Hail to the Hellcats.*

Then I looked across the field. The schedule said we were to play the Giants, but I had no idea they meant that literally. My confidence began to wilt. The adrenaline crawled out of my veins and went scampering down the yellow streak that had once been my spine.

On the first offensive series, I tried my best to "get in the way" of the 340-pound behemoth that loomed across from me. None of my tactics worked. My opponent looked like he had just escaped from a maximum security prison and had the attitude of an angry moose. He didn't go around obstacles– he went through them. After the first three plays, I was more trampled than the grapes of wrath. I spent the rest of the game on the sideline. On Monday, the coach informed me that my talent could best be used on "special teams."

This brings me back to the Starter® line of clothing. How could a person such as myself, and millions like me, morally and ethically wear the Starter® logo? After all, I only started one game in my entire life. Am I really qualified to wear a star? Will my friends and family (who know the truth) laugh at me behind my back?

Then I had a profound revelation. Why not create brands for non-starters? Self-help groups and counselors are always telling us to "feel good about ourselves – embrace who you are." With that in mind, I respectfully submit the following list. With these four exciting new brands, more Americans can look sharp, dress with pride, and have a clear conscience.

☺ **All-Star Reserve**: Created by a high-fashion designer, this line has the classy, dignified ring of twenty-year-old cognac. Wearing this brand says, "I could start every game if I chose to, but I'm being held back for special occasions. Just knowing I'm lurking on the sideline is enough to strike terror into the hearts of the opposition." Reservists abhor sweat and dirt. They usually fake an injury during practice and play only four or five snaps a game.

- ☺ **Second-Team Sensation**: Not quite as glamorous as the All-Star Reserve, but a gutsy, down-in-the-trenches, blue collar brand. Made for guys who spend all week at practice being a tackle dummy, but only get to play if the Starter is injured and All-Star Reserve comes down with a nasty hangnail.
- ☺ **Big Bad Bench Warmer**: This brand features a double layer of material on the seat of the pants for extra protection while "polishing the pine." Permanent grass and dirt stains are imbedded into the fabric to give the appearance that the wearer might have actually participated in a game at some point in his career (and I use that term loosely). Available only in sizes 3X and up.
- ☺ **Aqua Boy – Hydration Specialist**: Made for guys who love the smell of testosterone, but can't produce any of their own. Despite being hand-crafted from the best double-knit rayon in Sri Lanka, this brand is truly the Rodney Dangerfield of athletic apparel. If you want to be ignored, unappreciated, and treated with no respect, Aqua Boy can make you the modern eunuch of the "wanna be" jock scene.

Now that I've solved a major shopping dilemma for a huge portion of the world's male population, I can kick back on the couch with a couple of bags of corn chips, a quart of salsa, a six-pack of beer and enjoy the game.

Too bad I'm not coaching. I could teach those young offensive linemen a thing or two.

Last week, a couple of buddies stopped by to watch the game and we were all bragging about our glory days in high school. My wife happened to overhear the conversation and seized the opportunity to heap praise upon her hubby.

"Well, some things never change," she said. "When it comes to 'getting in the way' there's still no one that can beat Ol' Russ. As a matter of fact, he's taken it to another level."

Maybe I *can* wear a star after all.

Dreams of Mediocrity

Some people dream of being a professional athlete, a movie star, or the author of a *New York Times* best seller. What they don't understand is that once you make that bed of misery you have to lie in it. Fame and fortune brings celebrity status. You will no longer be able to hang out at Walmart, or browse the bargain bin at the thrift store without some maniacal fan recognizing you and begging for an autograph. Then they'll expect you to pose like a zoo animal while they snap several pictures with their cell phones to post on Facebook. No, thank you. I can live without that crap.

The old adage; "You can't buy happiness, but money makes misery easier to live with," may ring true, but why take a chance? Think about it. How important is it to have your face on the cover of the *Rolling Stone*?

Children in America are all fed the same line. You can grow up to be anything you want. The sky is the limit. All you need is a dream and the determination to put in thirty-nine and a half hours a day working your tail off to make it happen. Not so. Less than one percent achieve those lofty goals.

Dream of mediocrity, on the other hand, and the odds are in your favor. It doesn't require a lot of sacrifice or self-discipline, and you're never disappointed by failure. There's no pressure. You don't have to be good at anything – just resourceful.

In my position of lower middle management, I find it best to surround myself with bright, hardworking, ambitious young people. They're a creative lot and do a great job keeping me gainfully employed. The only problem is that some of them see me as a role model and insist on trying to sink to my level. I spend a great deal of precious time praising them, offering encouragement and support, and challenging them to accept the mantle of greatness they are destined to endure. Some of them are stubborn. I have to push, pull, and drag them – kicking and screaming – into leadership roles. Sometimes I even bribe them with promotions or pay raises. I'll do whatever it takes.

But these kids are smart cookies, and like Abe Lincoln said, "You can't fool all the people all of the time." They have observed my behaviors and habits and think that they can swing from the same vine as this old monkey. Sorry, Charlie. Mediocrity is not for everyone. It's an exclusive club, and those of us that enjoy its privileges want to keep it that way. I can't tell you how hard I worked or how long it took to become below average.

When we picked teams for kickball in elementary school, I always hid behind the taller kids hoping to get selected near the last round – just ahead of the fat boys and those that lacked physical and mental coordination. Once the game started, I was careful not to kick the ball too far or make outstanding defensive plays. That would have garnered attention and led others to believe that I had the skills and abilities to become an *athlete*.

I saw what happened to those poor saps. The teachers and coaches separated them from the rest of us, like chaff from wheat. They were driven mercilessly to perform at a high level. Good was never good enough. People were always hounding them about meeting expectations and living up to their potential.

The rest of us were treated with disdain or pity. The military-trained coaches and overachievers made fun of us, while soft-hearted angelic teachers would proclaim, "Bless his heart. He did the best he could." Many times I had to cover my face to hide a smile. On one occasion, after a particularly generous outpouring of sympathy, I tried so hard to suppress my laughter that tears ran down my cheeks. The teacher mistook this to mean that the big bad bullies had hurt my feelings. My reward was ice cream and cookies. I learned an important lesson about the value of mediocrity that day.

To give you a better understanding of how we underachievers think, allow me to clue you in on some of the major misconceptions of life. Supposedly, someone once said, "Necessity is the Mother of Invention." I don't know who that idiot was (probably another mediocre philosopher), but nothing could be further from the truth. Laziness, my friend, is the Mother of Invention.

The man that invented the wheel did not do so out of necessity. He could have easily carried his burden from point A to point B, but he was too damn lazy. I imagine he spent days, perhaps weeks or months, perfecting his invention. His not-too-bright half-brother finished moving the materials long before "Mr. Genius" completed his wonderful contribution to humanity.

Laziness aligns perfectly with another key tenet of mediocrity – procrastination. Never do today what you can put off until tomorrow. See how it fits like a hand in a glove? Here's an example of how I used procrastination to my advantage.

In my mid-twenties the dentist took one of those around-the-head x-rays and discovered my lower wisdom teeth were impacted. The film displayed both teeth lying on their sides facing the molars. His recommendation was that I have an oral surgeon cut those bad boys out. "It's a lot harder on you if you wait until you're older," he said.

The thought of forking over a handful of Ben Franklins, which I didn't have, and living on baby food and liquids for a week didn't fit my idea of a good time. Besides, they weren't hurting. So, I decided to put off the Chip and Dale impersonation as long as possible. I kept thinking, *what if I die in a car wreck before the teeth start giving me trouble? Then I would have gone through all that pain and expense for nothing.*

Last fall, almost thirty years later, he took new x-rays. The old wisdom teeth were still lying right where I'd left them. I mentioned I might need to get them removed someday.

"Nah," said the dentist, "at your age I wouldn't worry about it. If they were going to give you trouble, it would have happened before now."

"Good thing I didn't take your advice years ago," I said. We both got a good laugh out of it.

Procrastination is also handy around the house. Unfortunately, my wife frowns on the practice and is very persistent with frequent reminders regarding the chores she has assigned to me. She is not bashful about this in the least regard. Sooner or later she wears me down and I give in, but not until I've managed to postpone the task for a few months – and in some cases two or three years.

Early in my work career I discovered a profound truth: Those that can – do… and those that can't – become supervisors. What a wonderful revelation! I got down on my knees and thanked Almighty God right then and there.

It made perfect sense. Why would any intelligent business owner promote his most productive worker to a supervisory position? He might as well cut his own throat with a straight razor. Logic dictates that the best solution is to select a marginal performer who is reasonably competent for the job. Production won't suffer, and odds are good that the person hired to fill the open position will be more productive than the one you promoted.

All my years of being an underachiever were about to pay off. I let my mediocrity shine at every available opportunity. How could they not notice me? Here I was, right under their noses, stretching two hours of work into four.

Then one day my big break came. I was promoted to department supervisor and challenged to increase production by ten percent. This should have been easy, since there would be a natural gain just by removing me from the workforce.

I fell short. At my six-month evaluation I confessed to not meeting their expectations, but went on and on about all the new processes and procedures I had implemented and how hard I had tried to meet the goal. Moved by the genuine sincerity of my plea they agreed to keep me on. The sympathy card works every time.

I was right on the doorstep of lower middle management and didn't want to screw it up. People get suspicious if you start exceeding your goals, so I made sure they were aware of my many failures and shortcomings. Pay raises and promotions kept coming. Never underestimate the power of mediocrity.

All things considered, I've been very blessed. My skills are below average at almost everything I do, and I never miss an opportunity to employ laziness and procrastination if it keeps me from having to work.

Maybe the teacher was right. Dreams can come true.

The Incident

or

How I Discovered
Home Project Shock Syndrome (HPSS)

Have you ever wondered how diseases, syndromes, disorders, and other medical conditions got their names? Me neither. I just assumed it was a scientific process culminating in an "Aha!" moment by a group of well-respected physicians or scientists. Never in a million light years would I have imagined that a common layperson (who barely made passing grades in science) could discover and properly identify a previously unknown medical syndrome.

I don't mean to imply that Home Project Shock Syndrome, or HPSS, is an entirely new condition. Scientific evidence suggests that it has been around for centuries, quite possibly dating back to the creation of Eve. In the following thesis I will explain how I discovered HPSS, the symptoms of this dreadful disease, and effective methods of treatment (there is no known cure).

It is my firm belief that sharing this information with the medical community and the general public can save thousands of people from the heartache, suffering, and grief that I experienced – and if I am awarded the Nobel Prize for Medicine, that would be okay, too.

The event that led to my discovery of HPSS occurred the evening of May 25, 2010. My wife, Connie, and I have recollections of the 'incident' that vary in detail and perspective, but are similar in many respects. I've heard her version at least twenty-five times as she was questioned by EMTs, nurses, doctors, and anyone else who wanted the lowdown. She tells it exactly the same every time. There is no doubting the credibility of her testimony as star witness.

My memory of the event seems clear as well, but without some of the graphic details that make the 'incident' such a mystery, or in her words, "scary."

The day started out much like any other mid-week workday. We had planned to go to a meeting at the Goshen town hall to discuss a lot split of my parents' property. Like many rural hamlets across this great land, our local politicians had set up an intricate set of rules and regulations to make even the simplest of matters complicated and difficult to accomplish. I imagine they spend a great deal of time giving each other high fives after a unanimous vote to approve such legislation.

"This ought to slow down the process," they shout, breaking into a victory dance.

What's even more aggravating is that the property in question is not even within the city limits of this sprawling metropolis of 500. It lies in the so-called "growth area," which means they can lord it and rule over us, but we cannot vote in their elections.

In eighth grade history I was told that our Founding Fathers had done away with this type of tyranny, but unfortunately they failed to free Goshen, Arkansas when fighting for freedom and independence.

I'm a person who likes to plan and organize the day's events. I had been plotting sweet words and grateful phrases throughout the day to appease the tyrants and get the necessary paperwork approved and signed. Much to my surprise I received a phone call in the middle of the afternoon informing me that they were willing to accept the revised survey and that our presence that evening would not be required. (Another slow down tactic. The paperwork was to be rejected at least two more times.)

Blessed with what appeared to be a couple of hours of free time, I proposed to fall back to Plan "B ." This meant hoeing and fertilizing two rows of corn but, lo and behold, the heavens opened promptly at 5 pm and rain began to fall.

My third and final option was to replace a U-joint on a piece of farm machinery. It took about half an hour to remove the faulty part and I would pick up a new one the next day to finish the job.

By now it was almost 6:30. I mixed a Bloody Mary and invited Connie to join me on the front porch swing. A steady rain tapped peacefully on the metal roof above us.

Connie began explaining her grandiose plans for the garden shed "we" (feel free to substitute you – meaning me) could build incorporating the existing well house and arbor on the west side of our lawn. Her vision was practical – a dry enclosure for the tiller and garden tools, and an aesthetically pleasing lattice-covered wall with climbing flowers facing the house.

While she was explaining in intricate detail the beauty and functionality of this magnificent structure-to-be, I began to feel light-headed. (Whether or not this was caused by the proposed project was at that time undetermined, but I did share the possibility with many in the medical profession later that evening.) I remember telling myself to hold on in an effort to maintain self-control, but could tell that I was falling into a lesser state of consciousness. Spaced-out was the term we used in the 70s to describe someone who was dazed and confused. That shoe seemed to fit on this occasion.

Connie turned and saw me staring blindly ahead. My right hand shook and my left twitched. She waved her hand in front of my face, calling my name, but got no response. Placing her fingers on my throat, she tried to find a pulse. I cannot imagine the shock and panic that ran through her brain at that moment.

The next thing I knew, she was coming out of the front door talking frantically into the phone held against her left ear, while trying to dial the cell phone in her right hand. The thought of using two phones at once struck me as utterly ridiculous. Putting on my best George W. Bush smirk, I looked up and asked, "What in the world are you doing?"

"I've called 911. There is an ambulance on the way."

"Whatever for?"

Between bits of conversation with the emergency dispatcher on one phone and our neighbor Brenda on the other, she managed to tell me that I had been totally out of it. In her estimation I had suffered a heart attack or stroke and this was a life or death situation. She had called out the cavalry. Help was on the way.

Before I could formulate a sentence to inform her that none of this was necessary, Perry and Brenda arrived. Within minutes the local First Responders were flying past the mailbox while Brenda was screaming at the top of her lungs, waving both arms overhead from the driveway. Hell, with all its fury, had only begun to break loose.

The First Responders checked my vital signs and ran Connie and me through a series of forty questions that we were destined to endure over and over again for the next six hours. The EMTs arrived on the porch during Question twenty-three. They must have doubted the Responder's word for any of our previous twenty-two answers, for they insisted on re-asking every single question from the very beginning of the interrogation.

Despite my objections, and the fact that my vital signs were all running from normal to excellent, the vigilante mob that had assembled on the porch all agreed *somebody* needed to go to the hospital. I felt like the only black person at a Ku Klux Klan convention. All these people had been pulled from a comfortable evening at home – and by golly *somebody* was going to pay.

In the weeks that followed, I visited my family doctor a couple of times, took a treadmill stress test, and wore a heart monitor night and day for a full month. Highly paid specialists studied the test results and failed to find what triggered my "incident." Everyone had a theory – including me.

Mine was put to the test about a week after my release from the hospital. Connie and I had the opportunity to visit beautiful Omaha, Nebraska. The trip was part business, part pleasure. During the seven-hour drive from Fayetteville, there was ample time for pleasant conversation. I can't remember everything we discussed, but I was feeling just fine until Connie brought up a Home Project.

I could hear her talking, but the words were bouncing off the dashboard and tumbling to the floor. The deeper she dove into the details of what we could do the stronger the paralysis gripped me. Fortunately, she glanced over and noticed I was falling into a trance.

"Hey, are you all right?" she asked. "You're not having another spell, are you?"

Thankfully, changing the subject snapped me back to the land of the living. I worked hard to avoid lengthy conversations about Home Projects for the remainder of the trip.

My attempts to explain Home Project Shock Syndrome to the medical community have been met with skepticism. They don't seem to take my findings, or warnings, seriously. Some will grin and nod in agreement, but I can tell they are only trying to humor me. I suspect Lowe's and Home Depot are secretly paying them off.

Once I had gathered enough data to support my theory on HPSS, I set out to find a cure. You'd think with all the billions being spent every year researching stuff – like which fingernail polish looks best on monkeys and what color mood rings mice prefer – that I could get a measly couple of million for my work with HPSS. But, *nooo*! For some reason it doesn't qualify.

Armed with a whopping $12.38 (the remainder of my life savings after medical bills), I began my research. The first step was to find and study other victims of this terrible, debilitating disease.

That part was easy. The lumber yards, home centers, and hardware stores are full of them.

HPSS victims can easily be distinguished from regular construction workers (who get paid for their labor) by that glazed look in their eyes as they wander zombie-like through the store. Their wives guide them up one aisle and down another, providing creative ideas and helpful suggestions for the next four or five Home Projects they have planned. These poor helpless creatures' only response is a barely audible "uh-huh," or a painful moan at the cash register. What a horrible sight!

One day I decided to conduct an experiment. When the wife of a couple I was watching slipped away to catch the latest in kitchen flooring, I sauntered over to strike up a conversation with her husband. This poor gentleman was so stricken with HPSS that I barely even registered on his radar. I'm not even sure he knew what store he was in.

"Hey, Buddy," I said, in a soft, non-threatening tone. "Do you like fishing?" His left eye began to twitch. "How about hunting?" Now both eyes were blinking. "Would you like to spend a whole day on the golf course?" A broad smile graced his lips and the color in his face began to turn from gray to pink. The change was magical. I was elated! Now I knew how Al Gore felt when he invented the Internet.

If merely suggesting recreational activities could have such a positive effect on a patient's demeanor, could more improvement be expected if he actually participated in those activities? I couldn't wait to find out.

Unfortunately, my new friend's wife had other ideas. She came running out of the store, screaming and hollering when she saw me helping him into my truck.

"Bob, where do you think you're going? Who is this man?"

Then she turned her ire on me.

"You tried to kidnap my husband. I'm calling the cops!"

Everyone in the parking lot froze in their tracks and stared at us. She was still going off when the store manager came out to investigate the ruckus. I explained about HPSS and the seriousness of her husband's condition, but she was either in denial or just didn't care.

"Forget the cops," she told the store manager. "Call the nut house."

I'll never forget the despair on poor Bob's face as she led him to their car and shoved his broken spirit into the passenger seat.

The store manager didn't seem to appreciate my Good Samaritan effort either. He plastered my name and photo at every entrance and cash register under the heading **Banned for Life**. Word soon got around to the other home centers in town. I'm wallowing in celebrity status after becoming the first person to make America's Most Unwanted list.

After months of exhaustive research I have reached the following conclusions:

☺ HPSS is a real and verifiable medical condition

☺ Victims are primarily married males between the ages of 19 and 95

☺ Symptoms include, but are not limited to: dazed & confused appearance, gray facial complexion, grumbling or cursing in a low breath or whisper, and in severe cases– temporary loss of consciousness.

☺ Shock incidents can be triggered by detailed descriptions of proposed projects.

☺ Effective methods of treatment include, but are not limited to: fishing, hunting, golf, softball, camping, and other recreational activities.

☺ Sexual activity should be approached with caution as it is often a prelude to an actual home project.

Fortunately, HPSS is a manageable condition. For best results, I recommend applying one or more of the treatments above on a regular basis (twice weekly). Avoid lengthy conversations regarding proposed home projects, and by all means stay away from lumber yards and hardware stores. If you feel an irrepressible urge to visit a retail establishment, stop by a nearby sporting goods store or bait shop. You'll be glad you did.

Are You Healthy Enough to Go to the Hospital?

When I first discovered HPSS during *The Incident*, I became involved in a parallel, but highly important, research project: just how healthy do you have to be to go to the hospital?

When the First Responders arrived as a result of Connie's 9-1-1 call, my research began in earnest.

A gurney was brought to the porch. Large muscular men held my arms as I rose from the swing and advanced two steps to the waiting gurney. The remainder of the mob formed a circle around the immediate area to thwart any attempt at escape. After being strapped securely to the bed I was transported to a waiting ambulance for my 30-mph ride to the hospital.

Riding twenty-five miles while lying flat on your back is not an experience I'd recommend. The view out the tiny windows of the back door is rather odd. The scenery moves away from you. It's as if you are being sucked into some weird *Twilight Zone* dimension from which you may never return. I kept having vivid flashbacks of those movies where the ambulance hits a bump, the back door flies open, and the poor patient goes shooting into traffic, helplessly strapped to the gurney. This method of transportation is also eerily close to a hearse – need I say more?

My emergency-room nurse was a short man with glasses and a shaved head. He had broad shoulders and a barrel-chest, built like a middle-linebacker with a disposition to match.

After checking my vital signs a couple of times and another exhilarating round of forty questions, he handed me a plastic bottle and asked for a urine sample. "No hurry," he said, exiting the room. Three minutes later he was back.

"Where's my sample?" he demanded.

"I thought you said no hurry," I replied. "I've never peed lying on my back before. It's not that easy."

"Well, stand up if you need to. I don't care. You either give me a sample or I'm going to take it, and you know what that means."

Oh, boy. At that moment I was scared shitless. I'd never had to pee on demand before, but the visual image of a linebacker cramming a one inch rubber hose up my pecker was a real motivator. My penis immediately shrank to the size of a peanut shell and my testicles receded to somewhere in the upper regions of my body. I stood beside the bed, knees shaking, trying my best to wring a little water from my bladder.

"Please, Lord, give me three or four ounces to put in this bottle," I prayed. It seemed the harder I tried, the less I peed. Every time the sound of footsteps passed my doorway, I trembled in fear. Finally I relaxed enough to release a stream of precious liquid.

Much to my relief, he appeared satisfied with my donation. A broad smile graced his face and he whistled happily as he carried the golden elixir off to the lab.

Shortly after he left, a bespectacled female doctor arrived. So far, everyone I'd met at this place was wearing glasses. I began to wonder if we were at the Mr. Magoo Clinic of visually impaired medics.

Together we began to wade through the 40 question ritual, when out of nowhere she threw me a curve.

"Do you feel safe at home?" she asked. The first thought that flashed through my mind was murderers and thieves breaking in to pulverize and pillage. One look at Connie told me that wasn't what she meant.

In thirty-five plus years of marriage I've suffered through plenty of ass-chewings (most of which I deserved), but she never beat me with a stick or used demeaning language in an attempt to destroy my self-esteem.

There have been a few times when I thought she was trying to kill me with the home projects she dreams up. But after talking to other husbands I find that this is common behavior among married women. This method of torture is designed to accomplish two things. Number one, break the rebellious spirit of the male; and number two, make improvements to the home or property that would not otherwisc happen.

Dr. Four-Eyes seemed satisfied when we answered "No," but ordered a CAT scan and chest x-ray (just to be sure, I guess). The results showed no hemorrhaging in the brain and nothing abnormal in the lungs.

Nurse Linebacker returned from the lab with good news on the urine sample. In his opinion, they had no solid grounds to hold me and he expected my release to happen shortly.

But hold the phone! From out of nowhere came Dr. Dashingly Handsome. This pretty-boy reminded me of the commercial where the actor says, "I'm not a doctor, but I play one on TV."

He looked like he spent more time at a gym than in a hospital. His wavy black hair was held in perfect position by just the right amount of styling gel, and his glowing tan made him look like he'd just returned from a GQ photo-shoot in the Caribbean. His diagnosis made me the sickest I had been all night.

"Mr. Gayer, since we cannot accurately assess what caused you to have this episode, I believe we should keep you overnight for observation and run more tests tomorrow."

My immediate thought was, *"Yeah, Mr. Pretty-Boy, who died and appointed you Elvis?"* But with a little imagination and the right outfit, I could see him pulling it off.

Connie nodded like a bobble-head in agreement, and Dr. Handsome had my unhappy ass carted off to the third floor.

The first person I met there was a male nurse with the personality of a paperclip. He was extremely professional and all business. I don't think a whole room of comedians could have etched a smile on his stone face with a jackhammer. It was going to be a long night.

He hooked me up to a monitoring device with five leads attached to various points on my chest and stomach. This allows the staff to know if you are falling asleep so that they can come into your room and wake you on the pretense of taking your vital signs, drawing blood, or injecting a mystery serum. (I surmise that sleep deprivation is mandatory treatment for any illness at all hospitals. I expect water-boarding will soon be adopted as well.)

Shift change the next morning brought a new nurse and aide. Breakfast was served about 8 am, and was better than I expected. Your first meal must be the best, because the food went downhill from there.

A neurologist dropped by mid-morning and announced that I was scheduled for an MRI and an EEG. Shortly after noon they wheeled me downstairs to have a look at my brain.

The MRI technician was a pleasant lady in her early forties. She had me lie down on a narrow conveyor and wedged a thick chunk of foam on each side of my head. Next, she bolted a heavy plastic hockey mask just millimeters above my face. For the finishing touch, a tiny mirror was attached to the mask so that I could see my toes and the reflection of the machine in the window where the technicians sat watching (like that would keep you from feeling claustrophobic).

She inserted me into the machine with instructions to lie as still as possible. Not a problem. When you cram a twenty-four-inch-wide man into an eighteen-inch tube there isn't a lot of wiggle room.

For the next forty-five minutes I enjoyed all sorts of buzzing, beating, and clanging noises. I don't know if the machine really makes these, or if it's a soundtrack of a giant cash register keeping track of how much they're charging for the MRI.

My favorite was "six gongs." It sounds like someone hitting a propane tank with an aluminum baseball bat six times, followed by whacking a hollow wood block six times with a drumstick. This sequence repeats about forty times, non-stop. I tried to put lyrics to this magical rhythm, but nothing seemed to fit.

Upon my deliverance from the tube, I was greeted by a beautiful young woman. She helped me from the table to the wheelchair and began to escort me from the room. The fortyish lady returned and met us in the hall.

"I bet you thought I got a whole lot younger and prettier while you were in there, didn't you?"

"Well, I wasn't going to say anything," I replied, "but I was thinking, 'this dream is starting to get a whole lot better.'"

The young beauty turned me over to a couple of ladies across the hall for an EEG. For this test, they attached electrodes to my scalp to record the firing of neurons within my brain. To determine placement of the electrodes, they assigned vertical and horizontal lines on my head, like longitude and latitude on a globe. It takes about forty minutes to set-up a ten minute test. While they were dividing my head into quadrants, I explained how futile their attempts to capture useful data would be.

"Ladies, I've had CAT scans, MRIs, and people making me watch their fingers move from left to right. All tests of my brain have come back negative. Any neurons that may have survived will be bouncing off the walls at the speed of a tortoise crossing the Grand Canyon."

"You have a distinctive voice," said the one in charge, totally ignoring my medical prediction. "It reminds me of the Motel 6 guy . . .what's his name?"

"Tom Bodett," I replied. "A woman at work likes to recruit a crowd of new hires and have me recite the Motel 6 catch-phrase, 'We'll leave the light on for you.' It's starting to get old. Maybe I'll post some of *my* witty remarks on YouTube and everyone can tell Mr. Bodett *he* sounds like me. We could even call in sick for each other and . . . ."

"I think you're right," she said.

"You mean about Bodett?"

"No, the earlier comments about your neurons bouncing around like BBs in a barrel of Jell-O."

"I never said that."

"Close enough," she sighed. "Mr. Gayer, we're all done here. Ann will take you back to your room."

Early the next morning, another bespectacled technician wheeled a gigantic machine next to my bed to perform a heart echo test. He looked real spiffy in his bright red scrubs. I don't know if he was wearing red because we were on the heart floor, or to keep blood stains from showing on his uniform. In my opinion, plaids and prints work well for food stains, but who am I to give fashion advice to a man who wears pajamas at work?

The tech plugged in the machine and pressed a smooth round bulb against my chest cavity at various points, sending sound waves bouncing off the chambers of my heart. The rebounding waves were measured and recorded by graphs on the instrument panel and stored for a cardiologist to decipher between rounds of golf.

"Hello! Is anyone at home?" the machine would ask.

"Go away. You bother me," replied the heart.

"Are you all right? You're not beating very fast."

"Gimme a break. We're lying in bed, not running a hundred-yard dash. Why should I dance the rumba while the rest of the body is doing a waltz?"

"OK, but I'm going to have to tell the doctor you're being uncooperative."

"You do that. I'm sure he'll be impressed with your powers of perception."

The tech let the machine and heart argue while he recorded everything for posterity. Then he unplugged it from the wall and moved down the corridor to terrorize his next victim.

A couple of hours later the neurologist stopped by to re-affirm his conclusion that my brain showed no signs of a stroke or seizure. He avoided the word "normal," but stated he was confident in the results and no other tests of my noggin would be necessary.

By now, I'm midway through my second day of incarceration and every test has come back negative. As I walked through the halls of the third floor, patients with serious health problems were being sent home to rest and recuperate. I felt like a man who had been arrested and held without due process. *When do I get to see the judge? Am I eligible for parole or probation?*

I asked the nurse, "What kind of hospital is this? You send the sick people home and hold the healthy ones captive?"

"He's a little grumpy," said Connie. "Maybe an enema would improve his attitude." The nurse flashed a devious smile and nodded in agreement.

Getting out of this place was going to be a lot harder than getting in.

A couple of hours later the doctor made her daily visit. She was a tall woman with a figure like Olive Oyl. I knew she had the power to release me if could just convince her that I was healthy enough to return to society.

"I'm sorry, Mr. Gayer," she said in her whiny cartoon voice. "You can't go home until a cardiologist reads the results of your heart echo test and says it's okay. (I could just picture Dr. Popeye and Dr. Brutus slugging it out over who was going to deliver the report to Dr. Olive.) It's getting late in the afternoon, but I'll see if I can get him to look at it for you."

She must have turned on the charm (or flashed one of those toothpick legs), for at six that evening she returned with my release.

I was thrilled. My bad dream was finally ending. The nurse and I gathered my personal belongings, while Connie went to get the car.

As a final condition for my release, I was ordered to wait until an intern could retrieve a wheelchair and cart me to the curb. Evidently, it's bad for business if the public to see a patient walking out under his own power.

If you're planning on going to the hospital, make sure you're healthy enough to be a contestant on *Survivor*. Otherwise, you may not make it off the island alive.

The Path of Most Resistance

I have long ascribed to the notion that the best education you can get is a degree in Common Sense from the School of Hard Knocks. This college offers free tuition and you can earn thousands of credit hours by simply breathing and having a pulse. Books are optional, and there are no written exams.

On the downside, you couldn't cut class if you wanted to. You will be forced to endure thousands of boring lectures from hundreds of well-meaning individuals offering sage advice. They'll go on and on, revealing mysteries of the universe and other great truths designed to improve your miserable excuse for a life.

Do what I do – let 'em yak. You don't *have* to pay attention. Just smile, stick out your tongue and bob your head like the little doggie on the dash. You'll still learn something – I guarantee it. It's non-stop education.

You'd think a school that's been around since the beginning of time could boast of having produced dozens of famous alumni. Not Hard Knocks. In fact, their graduation rate is micro-scopically low. A lot of attendees *claim* to have a degree, but ask to see their diploma, or what they majored in, and they stutter like Porky Pig giving an inaugural address.

Some educators believe that the problem is related to Hard Knocks's reputation as a "party school." While it's true that the majority of the student body has been known to bend an elbow, most of them are simply thick-headed, stubborn, or downright rebellious. It's not that they are incapable of learning; they are just morally opposed to it.

One thing you can never accuse them of is laziness. You'd be amazed at the lengths these people will go to make the simplest of tasks difficult. Some have been known to circle the entire campus just to visit a friend across the street. This is also known as course #2247 – Taxi Driving 101.

Swimming against the current is a way of life in this end of the gene pool. No matter how many times the raging torrent slams them against unseen boulders, they refuse to change course. Driven by the irrepressible forces of nature, salmon travel hundreds of miles upstream every year to spawn, and in like manner so do these. Upon earning a Bachelor's Degree in Reproduction, many students go on to pursue a Master's. This guarantees millions of future enrollees at Hard Knocks.

Whether attending a major university or a small community college, kids are kids. Sooner or later someone is bound to get in trouble with the law. The School of Hard Knocks has taken a proactive approach in dealing with such unpleasant events. Administrators work closely with local law enforcement and judicial officers to ensure that students who have been convicted of a crime can continue their pursuit of higher education at a number of state run vocational/technical facilities, some-times referred to as prisons or penitentiaries.

Professors at Hard Knocks University apply old fashioned, tried and true, scientific principles when teaching. All core curriculum classes are taught by applying a fundamental doctrine, known as trial and error. Grades point averages are calculated based upon the number of failures and the severity of those mistakes. The logic being, that if you got it right the first time, you didn't really learn anything at all. Therefore, the more you fail the higher the score, and the more credits earned in the quest for Common Sense.

If you hope to graduate in less than thirty years (a daunting achievement by anyone's standards), you can orchestrate two or three major screw-ups every semester for extra credit. This may not make you any smarter, but it's sure to catch the attention of friends, relatives, insurance agents, and personal injury lawyers.

Potential employers frown upon applicants listing Hard Knocks University on resumes. Some have expressed reservations regarding the trial and error teaching method. They are concerned that the new hire will continue to adhere to the failure-equals-success mantra, and in so doing rise to the ranks of upper management, thus jeopardizing the careers of those in power. While this may seem like a reasonable assumption, I contend that the real problem is more cosmetic. It's all about image.

How can an institute of higher learning be taken seriously if it doesn't have a football team? This may seem unimportant to those who believe academics should be the primary function of a school, but if you're out on the golf course with the CEO and his cronies, it's a BIG DEAL, especially on college game day.

Corporate America loves college athletics. When you combine huge tax write-offs with a well-stocked liquor cabinet in a private skybox, it's a marriage made on the fifty-yard line.

Millions of dollars in sponsorship donations lay waiting to be harvested. All Hard Knocks has to do is find a few deep-pocketed alumni and hire a former Super Bowl coach. The team roster can be filled by recruiting a few of HKU's best from the aforementioned vocational/technical facilities. Televise try-outs for two dozen scantily clad, voluptuous cheerleaders with HARD KNOCKERS emblazoned across the front of their uniforms, and voila – instant credibility.

One thing the school doesn't have to worry about is establishing a fan base. It's easy to cheer for the red-headed stepchild. He rallies to take the lead, then turns to snatch defeat from the jaws of victory. We've all been there.

I made good grades in high school and was offered a scholarship, but after considerable thought, asked myself, "Why take the easy way out?" All that studying, going to classes, and preparing term papers would interfere with my social life. I had money in my pocket, a full time job, and was dating the hottest girl in town. Why mess with success?

Shortly thereafter, I took my first steps down that yellow-brick road known as the Path of Most Resistance. Enrollment at the school of Hard Knocks was so fast and easy I never knew when it happened.

Orientation took about six years, and the hazing never stops. I completed my freshman studies in just twenty-two years (not bragging – just a fact). At the rate extra credits are piling up, I hope to become a junior by age sixty-two.

The aging process has made trial and error learning more difficult. It's getting harder and harder to remember which things I've tried. The good news is I meet a lot of "new" old friends, sometimes the same ones two or three times a month.

College life has been good to me. Some lessons stick the first try. Others aren't so lucky. Friends and co-workers still offer suggestions and shortcuts to make my life easier. I put my fingers in my ears and hum the *Jeopardy* theme while they talk. They can tease me all they want about not having any degree of Common Sense, but I didn't come this far to give up now.

Donut Abuse

Have you ever received sex or drugs as payment for a donut? Have you ever paid anyone with sex or drugs in exchange for a donut?

These two examples from the blood donation questionnaire exemplify the seriousness of a horrible addiction that is sweeping our nation. A craving so strong and powerful it tears apart families, shatters homes, and destroys the lives of millions Americans each year. More dangerous than drugs, alcohol, prescription medication, or reruns of *Three's Company*.

Yes, I'm talking about donuts. Dee . . . Oh . . . capital N, nuts.

This highly addictive substance is made from flour-based dough, deep fried, and embalmed with a variety of sugary toppings to enhance flavor and boost its habit-forming appeal. Many abusers confess to having been hooked after only a single bite. Donuts come in a breath-taking bouquet of shapes, sizes, and tantalizing flavors to tempt even the most discriminating palate.

Bakeries, or Pastry Pushers as I like to call them, create clever nicknames such as Bismarck, éclair, Danish, or the crème-de-la-crème filled Long John. Don't be fooled. Each one is designed to enslave your taste buds, drain your pocketbook, and inflate your midsection to the point where they could write Goodyear on your sides and fly your bloated body over major sporting events.

Like other addictions, Donut Abuse tends to sneak up on the user. It starts innocently enough, but the result is always the same. Here's an example.

Janet works in an office. One day, Larry, a co-worker shows up with a twelve-pack of glazed artery-cloggers. Janet isn't really hungry, but she doesn't want to hurt Larry's feelings. So she has one – just to be social. The next day, Mike brings Bear Claws, then Brenda treats everyone to maple bars with nuts on top, and finally Robin shows up with the most addictive combination of all – chocolate covered chocolate donuts. After a few short days, Janet, a former carrot cruncher, finds herself craving donuts. She dreams about them at night and modifies her morning ritual to include a pit-stop at the neighborhood bakery just to salivate over the aroma of fresh, hot, heavenly treats.

Janet's co-workers huddle around the water cooler and whisper about the changes in her behavior. She is no longer a social butterfly who nibbles on one delicacy and then another. She becomes a wasp. Grabbing more than one donut without shame or embarrassment, she withdraws to the sanctum sanctorum of her cocoon (cubicle) where she uses her tongue in slow, deliberate strokes, painstakingly removing the icing before sinking her incisors into the very core of the trembling donut. Her body convulses in ecstasy. She exhales deeply and melts into her chair.

Poor Janet. It's all downhill from there.

Most abusers live in a world of denial. Sure, they'll admit to *liking* donuts, but believe they can quit at any time. "I only had *one* this morning," they brag. But the fragrance of powdered sugar drips from their breath at four in the afternoon. The desire for fresh fruit, vegetables, and whole grains becomes a distant memory.

Just the other morning, I was staring at a stoplight, hoping it would turn green before the century expired, when an SUV wheeled out of the convenience store parking lot and into the lane next to me. The driver, a semi-attractive woman about forty, appeared to be distracted by something in the passenger seat. She kept looking down, then at other drivers, as if to see if anyone was watching. Her behavior aroused my suspicion. I pretended to stare at the red light, all the while keeping her under close surveillance from behind my Foster Grants. Satisfied the coast was clear, she placed a large plastic bag on the steering wheel, opened it, and stared at the contents inside. Burying her nose in the bag, she closed her eyes and inhaled deeply.

Hmm . . . that looks like a donut bag. The thought had barely formed in my brain when she reached into the sack and extracted a cinnamon bun the size of a wagon wheel. I watched in horror as she tore into the pastry like a starving jackal gorging on the flesh of a tender, young gazelle. Bits of sugary glaze spewed from the bun with each bite like seed blown from a dandelion. Some landed on the dash, some on the steering wheel, but the majority took up residence on the front of her blouse.

It was not a pretty sight.

Studies over the past fifty years reveal that certain occupations run a higher risk of addiction than others. One in four office workers suffer from donut abuse compared to one in nine among factory and construction employees. Ironically, the profession with the worst track record is the one sworn to "protect and serve" the rest of us. That's right, our police force. The same men and women who put their lives on the line to keep our streets free of drugs, prostitution, and skateboards find themselves powerless in the presence of donuts.

Unfortunately, rather than reach out to help these poor people, the public has turned their addiction into the butt of a cruel joke. That's why you never see a uniformed officer standing in line at a bakery. They sneak in undercover or have someone make the "pick-up" for them, often forcing their own children to become Donut Runners in order to feed their habit.

"What can be done to help those who have a Donut Abuse problem?" you ask.

First of all, the public needs to recognize this disease for what it is – a serious addiction. These folks deserve the same treatment and rehabilitation options that are available to those who abuse drugs, alcohol, tobacco, and Facebook.

Donut Treatment Centers of America offers a thirteen-step program, commonly referred to as "The Baker's Dozen."

Dr. Orville Feeblemeister, founder and creator of the program, offers a list of symptoms family members should look for in determining if their loved one has become dependent on sugar-coated confections.

"Glazed eyes is a common denominator among addicts," says Feeblemeister. "Skin color may vary from powdery white to golden brown, with chocoholics displaying a dark circle around the mouth – and in extreme cases, on end of the nose – depending upon pastry preferences and the severity of the addiction."

In some cities, abusers, known as Donutheads, have banded together to form gangs such as the famous Krispy Kreme Klan (KKK). While some readily admit they have a problem, the majority of Treatment Center patients are there as a result of court ordered rehabilitation.

"Their initial reaction is anger and denial," states Feeblemeister. "Because of public perception, there's a lot of embarrassment and shame associated with donut abuse. The last thing they want is to spend two or three months locked in a treatment center because they can't control their obsession. That doesn't look good on a resume.

"They come rolling in here seeking a quick fix to their problem. Becoming addicted to donuts is easy and requires no conscious effort, but the road to recovery is like dining on an elephant and must be broken down into a series of small, bite-size morsels."

According to Feeblemeister, the first step is the most difficult. "No one wants to confess to being a slave to flour and sugar. Standing up in front of a group of strangers and publicly admitting that you are powerless against donuts takes a lot of courage."

The treatment center provides tools and training to help recovering addicts stay clean after they return to society. Telephone support is also available twenty-four seven at 1-800- NO DONUT.

"Avoiding temptation is the key," says Feeblemeister. "We recommend recovering addicts maintain a boundary of five hundred feet from any bakery or pastry shop. The human olfactory system is a powerful trigger. The aroma of fresh, hot donuts attacks the nostrils, crawls up the sinus cavities, and penetrates the desire lobe within the brain. The mouth begins to salivate. At that point, resistance is futile.

"With so many donuts on the streets these days, avoiding exposure is impossible. To combat the risk of scent-induced temptation, scientists in our lab developed a revolutionary set of nose plugs guaranteed to block the odor of fresh baked delicacies. These soft, comfortable inserts are tapered for a snug fit inside the nasal passage and come with, or without, nostril hair to provide that *natural* appearance. In fact, if it wasn't for having to breathe through your mouth, you wouldn't even know you had them in."

Corporations who once encouraged employees to gorge on donuts and coffee in hopes of a spike in productivity are now seeing health care costs double as a result of roly-poly workers who refuse to pursue a healthier lifestyle.

"We had so many Donut Addicts, our office pool became a wallowing hole for hippos," said the general manager of a large brokerage firm. "If it wasn't for the Diet Mountain Dew I.V., we wouldn't get anything done in the afternoon."

As a result of pressure from insurance companies, many businesses are now offering cessation programs to help employees kick the donut habit. Online enrollment is fast, easy, and discreet. Those who sign up receive regular phone calls from trained counselors offering encouragement and support, a packet of printed materials containing tips and tricks, and coupons for patches, gums, and donut substitutes.

"No matter how strong you think you are, there are going to be times when you are vulnerable," says a former addict, who wishes to remain anonymous. "Just because you slipped and ate a maple bar at a training seminar doesn't make you a failure. Those things happen. It's like being thrown from a stick-horse. Dust yourself off and climb back in the saddle."

With Donut Abuse reaching epidemic proportions, health food lobbyist are pressuring Congress to pass Donut Control measures that would ban certain pastries and require background checks for purchases over one dozen. This has brought protests from the National Donut Association (NDA), who maintains that such laws violate the U.S. Constitution and infringe upon the people's God-given right to life, liberty, and the pursuit of sugar-coated confections.

I fall into that wishy-washy well of individuals who can't think and scratch our rear at the same time. We've witnessed the devastating effect of Donut Abuse on family and co-workers, but we're not ready to throw out a perfectly good, half-eaten cinnamon roll with yesterday's cooked-down decafe. The rights of social dunkers must be protected.

With no easy solution in sight, the best thing we can do is educate our children on the dangers of Donut Abuse. One way to do this is by modeling self-discipline and proper pastry etiquette. Kids should be taught to treat donuts with the same cautious respect normally reserved for rattlesnakes and used car salesmen. Never eat the first or last donut without expressed written consent from the person who bought them.

By establishing a few simple rules and easy-to-follow guide-lines, we can teach young people how to peacefully coexist with pastries without becoming slaves to dependency. For this to be successful, adults are going to have to step up to the plate and limit children's exposure to these habit forming substances.

That's why I've started a "save the children" campaign to create a donut-free environment. You can support the program by dropping off dangerous donuts, crème-filled artery cloggers, and sinful cinnamon rolls at the handy disposal station located on the left corner of my desk.

I assure you they will be destroyed immediately.

Courting the Fat Vote

To all those who send, receive, enjoy, or gag at the visual images in the "People of Walmart" emails, be forewarned. A recent newspaper headline declared, "Walmart Pledges Obesity Fight."

As part of their agreement with *Partnership for a Healthier America*, Walmart has vowed to open new stores in USDA-designated food 'deserts' to serve urban and rural markets. Other outlets will be converted into 'food oasis stores' that will sell whole fruits and vegetables, pre-cut fruit salads, and green salads.

Goodbye Twinkies, Ding-Dongs, candy bars, elf-cookies, potato chips, and other goodies laden with fat or dredged in sugar. Hello tofu, raw veggies, and rice cakes.

If Walmart goes on a health kick, where will the obese shop? Who will defend their right to eat unhealthily? Will fattening food fall into the same cancerous spiral that choked the cigarette industry into a slow, painful coughing fit?

Many employers have increased insurance premiums for those who use tobacco. Future health care increases will be based on Body Mass Index. Expect to see designated "munching areas" set up for employees who are addicted to candy, sodas, and other high-calorie foods. Imagine the cruel jokes from carrot-crunchers, ridiculing the poor Lard-o in the "Fat Shack" who dove to the ground retrieving a runaway M & M. My side hurts just thinking about it.

Lawmakers will seize the opportunity to generate a whole new tax revenue stream – akin to the 'sin tax' on tobacco and alcohol. It would not be politically correct (nor polite) to call it the "Fat Tax," so they'll have to come up with something less offensive to the obese. How does the Tubby Toll sound?

According to Walmart, this is a result of Michelle Obama's *Let's Move* campaign aimed at childhood obesity. While this appears to be a noble cause, born of good intent, Mrs. Obama failed to consider that two-thirds of American voters are clinically obese. Our nation's tendency to overeat, sport bulging love-handles and double-wide derrieres, extends beyond social and economic backgrounds, and does not discriminate on the basis of race, gender, or religion. Let's face it. This is America – land of the free and home of the Fat & Sassy.

After sizing up the candidates in the 2012 Presidential race, it's hard to find someone I can stand behind. After all, do we really want some skinny little stick-person trying to represent our nation? Who's going to take them seriously? (I can hear Russia laughing all the way to the buffet.) America needs someone who will throw our collective weight around when dictating policy to those foreign scoundrels. I want a president with the courage and intestinal fortitude to take a serious bite out of the issues that threaten freedom and our God-given right to life, liberty, and the pursuit of the perfect cheeseburger.

This brings me back to the original point of this article; do we really want "People of Walmart" emails featuring skinny, dried-up, little health nuts? Just think how repulsive it would be to see photos of a perfectly proportioned fitness model, wearing oversized gym shorts and a loose fitting T-shirt, shopping for fruit-salad? B-o-r-i-n-g.

How is *that* going to make me feel better about myself?

Don't get me wrong; my heart bleeds for those poor middle-aged men in miniskirts, the ninety-year-old cougars in leopard-print spandex, and the Two-ton Tessies wearing a size eighty-six, hot-pink, string bikini with "Color Me Sexy" emblazed across the rear. I cringe at the sight of their sad faces.

But we can't just turn our backs on these people and pretend they don't exist. That would be like ignoring the cries of the homeless, shunning lepers, or pretending no one is home when Jehovah's Witnesses knock on the door.

CLASSIC-
The "New" Old

As a person who likes to play with words (i.e. arranging them in nonsensical order), I've always been intrigued by the way Americans take a particular word or phrase and transform it into something totally unrelated to the original definition. Sometimes, we fall so in love with a word (and all its variations) that we begin to use it as a noun, verb, adverb, adjective, and practically every other grammatical term we failed to memorize in eighth grade English.

The wonderful thing about these words is how flexible they are. A perfect example is the one syllable "F" word. When I first became acquainted with this word (during the early stages of puberty) the common definition was simply copulation– to engage in sexual intercourse. I immediately took to it. Only four letters, easy to spell, easy to pronounce, and everyone knew exactly what you were talking about. What made it even more fun was that it was forbidden. You could get paddled, have your mouth washed-out with soap, or suspended from school for saying it. Even writing it on paper or bathroom walls was a no-no. Talk about censorship!

I've known people who were so in love with the "F" word that they wanted to use it in every sentence, sometimes three or four times! By adding suffixes, such as "er," "ed," or "ing," the word becomes so flexible you can use it in anywhere in a sentence, and make it mean anything you want. Once you're comfortable with these, add "F*ed-up" and people will know that you are a Master of the English F*-ing language.

Now, let's move on to the word, "Classic". After all, that is the primary topic of this report.

According to my 1981 Webster's New Collegiate Dictionary, the Latin word *classicus* was an adjective referring to the highest class of Roman citizens. If you want to use "Classic" as a noun, an example would be an ancient Greek or Roman literary work, or a traditional event. Based on these definitions we can assume the word has been around a long time – probably not as long as the "F" word, but still several centuries.

For the first thirty years of my life, I rarely heard "Classic" used. Occasionally, a college professor or English teacher would encourage students to read the "classics," or some sportscaster on TV would be talking about the Bob Hope golf tournament, but that was about it. The word "Classic" was having difficulty competing in daily conversations with words that implied sexual activity.

The turning point came in April of 1985. The makers of Coca-Cola® decided to abandon their ninety-nine-year-old secret formula and unveiled "New" Coke. It was failure of epic proportions. A firestorm of consumer protest quickly convinced Coke executives that something had to be done. People liked the old stuff better. But how do you go back? You don't want to call it "Old" Coke. That would make it sound like it had been sitting around in a warehouse forever. What's an upscale word for old that will sound classy and appealing to the public? Hmm . . . I don't know . . . how about . . . Classic?

In the blink of an eye, "Classic" was pulled from the shadows of obscurity and thrust into the limelight of fame and fortune. Television, radio, and billboards proclaimed the wonder and greatness of "Classic." Once out in the open, "Classic" took the world by storm. Soon people were referring to old music as "Classic" Rock, Jazz, or Country. Movies and books that were flops became best sellers because someone called them "Classics."

My beat up, gas guzzling, 1972 Chevy can be referred to as a "Classic Muscle Car" instead of a worn-out piece of junk.

Here are a few other examples of how you can substitute "Classic" for the word "old" in everyday conversation.

My cousin Jerry recently turned sixty-five, which officially qualifies him as "Old." Without applying modern terminology, I might have referred to him as an Old Fart, Codger, or Geezer. Now, I can proudly introduce him as a Classic Fart, Classic Codger, or Classic Geezer, all of which would be appropriate considering that he is indeed an ancient individual. See how much more respectful and dignified these titles sound?

Consider the phrase, "dirty old man." This seems to imply that the male being described is prone to some form of sexual perversion. However, if we change the middle adjective, our subject becomes a "dirty Classic man." Notice what a difference one word makes? Now, we envision a fine fellow who simply fails to practice proper personal hygiene.

"Classic" is also gender friendly. When referring to the gentler sex, I recommend using it as a noun – simply stating, "She's a 'Classic.'" This provides the listener an opportunity to inject a word of their choosing at the end of this statement to more clearly define their perception of the female in question.

I hope this dissertation on proper use of the word "Classic" has been helpful to you. Be thinking about situations where you can apply this new-found knowledge in daily conversation. I guarantee your friends and family will be appreciative of your mastery of this wonderfully descriptive word. Especially those like Jerry, who are really, really, really F*ing OLD.

The Ultimate Instructional Guide
How to write "How To" books

While perusing the aisles of my local bookstore, I couldn't help but notice the wide variety of genres and subject matter available. If you enjoy fiction, they stock a huge selection of romance, mystery, fantasy, and even erotica to tease the most curious mind. They also carry an array of well-researched biographies, historical, and non-fiction books. Best sellers are promoted on beautiful end-cap displays, adorned with glorious graphics to convince you that each one is a "must read."

My personal favorites, and by far the most dominant genre in terms of numbers in print, are the "How To" books. I like to refer to them as "Instruction Manuals for the Ignorant."

When I think of all the months of exhaustive research and tireless nights spent pounding on the keyboard, I am humbled by the thoughtfulness of the men and women who go to all this trouble just for me.

They don't even know who I am. Yet, they sense my lack of aptitude and put their busy lives on hold long enough to author volumes of self-help literature, covering subjects I didn't know even existed.

My wife has scores of books on gardening, crafts, and health-related topics. I have books and magazines intended to improve my fishing and hunting skills, along with those offering advice on writing and tips to increase my odds of actually getting something published.

Our library at work contains volumes of instructional information on teamwork, leadership, successful negotiations, and how to be a better manager. These are filled with clever catch phrases to help the reader remember specific points through repetition.

Some authors in this genre have actually held real jobs. Most however, built a career by writing "How To" books and offering consultant services. They convince corporate executives that forcing thick-headed employees to sit through multiple-day seminars is a good business investment.

I've had the displeasure of attending a good many of these wonderful training experiences. It's paid time away from your regular job, free lunches, and you get to hang out with other employees you don't see too often. Afterwards, we each write a paragraph about how much we learned and how we will put this new-found knowledge to use for the betterment of the company. Everybody goes home a winner – one of them very well paid.

As a fledgling writer, I must confess my envy of the "How To" author. What a noble profession. I can think of nothing more gratifying than building a bridge to enlightenment for those of us who grope in the darkness of ignorance. How can I ever repay such a debt?

Then it came to me. Surely there must be a topic where I can offer some expertise. I scoured the aisles of the bookstore and surfed the web. Frustration mounted as weeks turned into months. Night after sleepless night, I lay awake wondering, "What is the missing 'How To'?"

Finally, I threw in the towel. Maybe God didn't want me to help people in this way.

One morning, while shuffling through a pile of books on the coffee table something caught my eye. Hidden at the bottom of the stack were two instructional manuals. They were fanned out in such a way that I could only read part of the title of each book. The one on the bottom said, *How to Write* . . . , and the book on top was entitled, *The How to Book of* . . . .

It was a Moses moment. A warm glow started at the tips of my fingers and slowly crept up both arms to the back of my neck. My face flushed. My ear hairs tingled. Despite my protests, whining, and confessions of inadequacy, there was no getting out of it. I had been chosen for the monumental task of writing the ultimate instructional guide: *How to Write "How to" Books.*

Normally, I procrastinate at least a couple of weeks before beginning any new project. But this time, I felt compelled to begin work immediately. It was like an unseen hand grabbed me by the shirt collar and threw me into the writer's den.

The work wasn't easy. I chiseled, scratched, and wrestled with the words. Round after gut-wrenching round we fought. The air was filled with flying debris from unnecessary adverbs and tired clichés. My fingers ached from hammering out axioms. Sweat poured from my brow and peppered the sacred manuscript like droplets of falling rain.

I lost all concept of time. The only thing that mattered was completing the task. When at last I emerged, tattered and worn, my wife cocked her head and shot me the most awful look.

"How long has it been since you had a haircut?" she asked. "Your beard is hanging down to your navel. You need to clean yourself up. And why are you walking around in that ridiculous robe with a tablet under each arm?"

It was one of those situations where being truthful would just lead to questions about my sanity, so I changed the subject.

"It's dark in here. Why are the lights so low?"

"I was afraid you'd see your shadow, and we've have six more weeks of writing. You need to come out and experience the real world once in a while."

From past experience, I knew it was pointless to argue or try to explain. She wouldn't understand – or really care. I'm always selfishly depriving her of quality time by sneaking off to a nearby computer to write the next great non-selling story of the unpublished world.

I shot her a sly little grin, and thought about all the abuse Moses took when he came down from the mountain. Why should I expect to be treated any differently?

"What have you been working on all this time?" she asked.

"I was appointed to write a manual entitled, *How to Write 'How to' Books*."

"Say what? Appointed by who?" She leaned back slightly and scrunched her eyebrows.

"God . . . God wanted me to write this. He gave me the words to put on these tablets. Rules that will help people avoid serious mistakes. By following these commands they can better serve others."

I watched her fingers sneak nimbly across the kitchen counter toward the phone. My sanity was no longer in question. She had the funny farm on speed dial and her index finger glued to the call button.

"You have lost your freakin' mind." She bit off the words in a slow, deliberate manner, as if they were being chopped from a block of wood. "First you throw out this ridiculous Abbott and Costello title. Then, you try to make me believe it was divine intervention? What have you been drinking?"

"Nothing . . . I swear. Before you pass judgment, just read the tablets. It's not the sorry stuff I usually write. It's inspired – you'll see"

She let out a long sigh, picked up her reading glasses, and sat down at the kitchen table. I slid the manuscript in front of her and leaned back against the refrigerator to watch her expression as she read.

"I can't read with you looking over my shoulder," she said. "All this hard work has made you smell like a pig. God wants you to take a shower." She looked up with a sarcastic little smile and batted her eyelashes.

On my way down the hall, I could hear her reading the commandments in her best Charlton Heston impersonation.

Know Thy Audience – Whether you are writing a book on making snowmen out of cotton balls, or how to perform brain surgery with a Swiss Army knife (while holding a flashlight in your teeth), it's important to remember who is laying down their hard-earned cash to purchase your powerful insight and expertise. I recommend you target simpletons to start with and work your way up. A great example of this gold mine is the "How to for Dummies" series. You won't find many of these lying on coffee tables, but I guarantee there are millions of these bright yellow books hidden away in attics and closets around the world. If you see somebody sneaking around the self-help section, dressed incognito and wearing dark glasses, it's safe to assume they are shopping for a "Dummy" book.

Thou Shalt Use Photos and Illustrations – Whoever said, "A picture is worth a thousand words," wasn't just yakking to hear their head rattle. Many people are visual learners, especially those from Missouri. The reader may have received your book as a gift. They may not even be literate (see Commandment I). Remember, the more pictures you use, the fewer words you have to write.

Repeateth Thy Clever Catch-Phrase Often – As a rookie writer, you were chastised for using the same words too frequently in your story. Well, you're not writing a story now chump – so throw that rule out the window. You are a teacher and this is your text book. Memory retention is dependent upon repetition. What did I just say? Memory retention is dependent upon repetition. See how easy that is? Good. Let's move on.

Praise Thy Reader - My wife's uncle owned a car dealership. He was fond of saying, "I don't want to sell a customer one car. I want to sell them every car they'll ever buy for the rest of their lives." What makes this philosophy work? Exceptional customer service. Your reader made a wise decision choosing your book. Don't be bashful about telling them how smart they are. Keep it up, and they'll tell their friends what a great author you are and how much they loved your book.

Summarize Thy Wisdom – You have given the reader a great deal of information. Now that they've chewed up and digested every tasty morsel, how do you expect them to retain all that new-found knowledge? In your final chapter, it's time to grab the bull by the tail and look it in the eye. Condense everything from the preceding chapters into a single page that can be torn out and stuffed into a shirt pocket. The proverbial quick-reference/recipe for success.

Compelling be Thy Title – Tell me in six words or less why I should pick up your book and look inside. You're competing with dozens of authors who've written on the same subject. What makes your instruction manual superior? Titles in this genre tend to fall into two categories. Number one, appealing to the lazy, such as; *It's Fun, and So Easy*. Number two, the authoritative method; *Cause I Said So – Damn It!*

Thy Cover Shalt Catch the Eye – You've heard the old expression, "It's not what you say – it's how you say it." The book cover and spine are your billboards. You may have a killer title such as; *Tips for Judging Bikini Contests*, but without great cover art, your book will languish on the shelf, covered with cobwebs and dust. Think how sad it would be to deprive potential readers of such a fine piece of photo-journalism.

Find Thyself a Witness – The back cover is reserved for coveted testimonials from respected authors, or publications, who you have bribed to sing the praises of your book. Be choosy. Use only credible sources. This can be especially effective if the witness is an expert in the field you are writing about. If your Mom says something particularly nice about your book, and you want to use her quote, have her sign it Eleanor Roosevelt. Dead people never lie about good books.

Waste Not Thy Flaps – The parts of a book jacket that fold inside the front and back cover are referred to as flaps. Why they aren't called lapels makes absolutely no sense to me. Think of the front flap as your thirty-second ad to convince prospective buyers they can't live without your book. Give them just enough juicy meat to make them drool, without giving way the whole ham. The back flap should contain a short biography and picture of the author. If you are homely (trying to be nice here), consider other options. I suggested to Stephen King that he go with a caricature. Now, he won't speak to me or return my messages. Those literary types can be so sensitive.

Promote Thy Book – Have you ever heard of the movie, *The Wrath of Grapes* (not to be confused with *The Grapes of Wrath*)? Rumor has it a famous producer spent millions of dollars making a top-notch horror film about a Fruit from the Loom gone bad. The Purple Cluster turned on his under-wear sidekicks and chopped them into fruit salad. When detectives started snooping around, he threw the dismembered bodies into a blender in an attempt to smooth over his crime. Lots of puree and gore. Unfortunately, they spent their entire budget making the film and were too broke to promote it. What a shame. I'm sure it would have been a box-office hit or a cult classic favorite. Don't let this happen to your book.

I returned from the shower just as she finishing reading.

"Well, what do you think?" I asked, anxious as a kid on Christmas morning.

"You're right," she said, peering over her readers. "It *is* better than most of the stuff you write. I guess God does work in strange and mysterious ways.

Intellectual Futility

Like millions of other Americans, my name is on 342,751 mailing lists entitling me to thousands of "special offers" not available to the general public. This leaves a total of seven people in the United States, Mexico, and Canada who are not given the opportunity to subscribe to magazines, purchase unwanted life insurance, or sign up for ten new credit cards per day at ridiculously low rates.

Sometimes I wonder how these folks got left out and what puts me in the elite crowd. Did they simply fall through the cracks, or were their names intentionally omitted because of a sin one of their ancestors committed three generations ago? How do they feel about being ostracized by giant marketing entities who deprive them of the joy of harassing phone calls and Santa-size bags of direct mail? Are they angry, bitter, and emotionally scarred?

It must be embarrassing when their friends and neighbors whisper, "Hey, have you heard about Joe? That poor guy doesn't get *any* special offers."

"Yeah, I know. It's so sad. I really feel for him. Wonder what his great-grandmother did?"

The only way it could be any more humiliating is if the paparazzi followed Joe around, posting his picture on the cover of every gossip rag in the grocery store. His photo right next to one of the Kardashians under the headline, JOE DENIED SPECIAL OFFERS!

Fortunately, that's a problem I'll never have to deal with. The marketing gods have gone out of their way to make sure my name is on the top of the list for everything from collectible dust bunnies to mail order cheese curds. My wife has been selected from the masses by *Publishers Clearing House* and *Reader's Digest*. Every year they threaten to reward her with huge sums of cash if she'll just respond immediately. Six months and twenty-two mailings later she's inched ever closer to becoming a grand prize finalist. At this point, we slip into our Sunday-best and wait for the Prize Patrol film crew to come rolling into our driveway.

Then, without warning, the mailings stop.

Evidently, there's something in the rules stating that in the event of a one-hundred-and-forty-seven-way tie the contest administrator gets to take the money and a mistress of his choice on an extended vacation to a tropical paradise somewhere in the Caribbean. I hope they have plenty of magazines on that island. If not, we've got a few hundred I would gladly donate to help them pass the long hours lounging in beach chairs, nursing buckets of Coronas.

While he's gone, they appoint a new administrator (a much sought after position) and begin the contest all over again. Meanwhile, hope springs eternal for the millions of Americans whose only retirement plan hinges on becoming a mail-order millionaire.

Another group of special offers that I'm privy to includes death and dying. First you start with a packet of low-cost life insurance plans, followed by the ever popular pre-paid funeral arrangement. And, if you act now, they'll throw in a reverse mortgage, turning the entire deal into a plan they call the "Moment of Mortality Trifecta."

This marketing ploy reminds me of the advertising line-up they ran on my mother's soap operas. First they'd start with constipation or diarrhea (take your pick), followed by hemorrhoid medicine, then Mr. Whipple would show up with the Charmin. Proving once and for all that a job is never finished until the paperwork is done.

As a member of lower-middle management, I get pounded with all kinds of offers at work. Phone calls pour in daily from telemarketers around the globe who want to continue my FREE subscription to magazines I've never heard of and they can't pronounce. The conversation goes something like this;

"Goot morning, Mr. Dayer. My name is Harvey (short for Ninjay Fuqua) and I'm calling to renew your circumcision to *Colon & Bladder* magazine. Dis call may be monitored to enjoy your complete dissatisfaction. Now, if I may ass you a few questions to confirm your conscription. Your name is Rashell Dayer, correct?"

"Yeah, that's close enough."

"And de name of your company is Tasty Fooze?"

"That's right."

"And I have your mailing address to be Four-Six-Nine Vest Gohmer Road in Frozen Lake, Arizona. Is dat correct, sir?"

"Actually, the lake never freezes, but feel free to send the magazine there."

"Hookay, sir. Tank you merry much. Only a few more questions, please. To confirm that we spoke—what was your mudder's maiden game?"

"Scott."

"Snot. Hookay, berry goot,sir. Tank you again, Mr. Dayer and employ your free prescription to *Colon & Bladder* magazine. Goot day."

It's a waste of breath to tell these people you're not interested. They're going to send the magazine anyway. My advice is to take a handful of sedatives and brace yourself for a trip down *Colon & Bladder* lane.

Another area of constant harassment is training opportunities. Once they have your email address and fax number, it's like you have a giant bull's-eye painted on your mid-section. Since I'm a rather broad fellow, my target area tends to be a little larger than most, but let me assure you, these folks can knock a chigger off a gnat's ass if it's hiding on the dark side of the moon.

Now, don't get me wrong. I'm not totally opposed to training. Without it, millions of people would still be running around with stains on the front and back of their pants. And what about all those pre-adolescent girls whose young boobies would have gone astray had it not been for those special bras designed to correct errant boob behavior. And how many people would've never learned to ride a bicycle without two extra wheels to provide added self-confidence?

So you see, there *is* a place for training. I'm just not sure it has anything to do with work. Isn't that supposed to be a mindless activity where they just use you from the shoulders down? I shudder to think what would happen if everyone in the workforce was fully trained and competent. It would eliminate the need for lower-middle managers. Who would guys like me rule and lord over?

Three to four times a day, I receive communication from training companies offering classes, seminars, audio conferences, webinars, and get this—even hardcopy books—for us old geezers who are swimming upstream against the electronic age. The advertising copy claims they can turn sock puppets into great leaders, infuse deaf mutes with powerful negotiating skills, and teach terrified introverts how to cope with stubborn old curmudgeons (such as yours truly).

What they fail to include is a four-page disclaimer listing possible hazards and side effects, which would read something like this: Students enrolled in this course have been known to develop migraines, nosebleeds, nausea, vomiting, and involuntary bowel movements. Do not take this class if you are pregnant, can become pregnant, or have a family history of alcoholism. Avoid contact with normal people for at least twenty-four hours after completing this course to allow over-inflated egos to shrink to normal size. Failure to do so could result in a pummeling of insults, acts of physical violence, and in some cases—even death. Should any of these symptoms occur, discontinue training and get to the nearest psychiatrist or voodoo doctor immediately.

One of the new courses they are promoting is entitled Emotional Intelligence. The name itself is an oxymoron of epic proportion. I didn't know it was possible to stand those two words side-by-side without a fistfight breaking out in mid-sentence. It was enough to pique my curiosity. So against my better judgment, I opened the email and read more.

According to the ad copy, by attending this course, I'd be giving myself the best gift of all—control over my emotions *and* the power to manipulate others—my new secret weapon for success. Mastering Emotional Intelligence, or EI as they like to call it, would give me a sixth sense for how others are feeling. I'd be able to detect and decipher emotions in faces, pictures, voices, and even cultural artifacts at the local museum. An arrowhead would no longer be a sharpened stone, but an indicator of how a Native American was feeling on a particular day. Perhaps he was upset because his wife was on the warpath or his mother in-law had worn out her welcome at their wigwam.

Next, I'd learn to reason with my emotions. This means instead of having a wrestling match like we usually do, we'd sit down and hash things out in a calm, logical manner without cursing or name calling.

I just have one question. If this technique is so effective why is the instructor in the brochure wearing a striped shirt with a whistle dangling from her neck?

After learning to perceive and interpret nonverbal signs I'd be able to fully capitalize on my changing moods to best fit the task at hand. For example, I could harness my EI powers to teach that smart-ass little twit in the next cubicle the meaning of fear by hiding a few rubber snakes or starting a romantic pen-pal relationship in his name with a convicted rapist who will soon be released from prison.

If I enroll now, my company can send a second person for only $99 more. That's scary. The last thing I want to do is work with someone who's been through *this* course.

To repay the corporate world for all the wonderful learning opportunities they've bestowed upon me, I've develop my own training program. It's designed for those gullible misfits who want to expand their knowledge and take home a pretty certificate with a gold embossed seal next to their name. Participants will spend an entire day fiddling with square pegs, swallowing bitter pills, and performing other idiomatic expressions such as paying with an arm and a leg or having a cow.

Enroll today and experience the joys of "Intellectual Futility."

Irritable Vowel Syndrome

My nouns and verbs don't always agree. Fistfights have been known to break out in mid-sentence. – Russell Gayer

Do you have a problem enunciating two-syllable words? Has a therapist compared your speech pattern to the guttural grunts of a Neanderthal with a mouthful of Novocain? When you type an email, do all the consonants run to one side of the page and quiver in fear? If so, you may be suffering from Irritable Vowel Syndrome.

Irritable Vowel Syndrome (IVS) strikes millions of people around the globe, from young children scrawling their very first word with an oversized crayon to seasoned authors pounding out the next New York Times best seller. If you make out a grocery list, type an email, or scratch graffiti on the walls of a public restroom it's only a matter of time until you suffer from a serious attack of IVS.

Known in polite circles as The Conversation Killer or the King of Communication Confusion, IVS attacks a little-known section of the brain called the Bouche de Toilette, or Potty Mouth Quadrant. Scientists have yet to pinpoint the exact cause of IVS, but experts agree that repeated exposure to political ads, abusive employers, and nagging mothers-in-law tend to further aggravate the condition.

Consonants can be naughty at times, but in a good-natured, playful way. There's nothing evil or mean-spirited about their intent. A great example of this is the letter H and the M & M brothers, who often join forces to form "Hmm." This expression can be interpreted a variety of ways depending upon the inflection of the speaker.

Let's say you're watching your favorite football team on TV. They're down by four points, but have the ball on the two-yard line. Its fourth down with seven seconds left on the clock. The center is about to snap the ball when your wife steps between you and the television. She's wearing a skimpy negligee.

"Well, what do you think?" she asks, with a grin the size of Texas.

You tilt your head to one side and the phrase, "Hmm" escapes your lips. This is where the inflection part becomes critical. Screw up here and you'll be eating Bolo without the aid of a spoon and sleeping with Fido in a plastic igloo.

But if you play your cards right – by wiggling your eyebrows, leaping to your feet, and throwing both arms around her – you can watch your team score the winning touchdown over her shoulder and break into your little victory dance without her ever becoming suspicious.

Be sure to pat her on the butt a few times while jumping up and down, screaming, "Yes, yes, yes!" This sends a clear message that you really love her little outfit and the gal inside it. Now, you've earned a five-course meal and an evening of romance, not necessarily in that order.

Vowels, on the other hand, are like ruthless outlaws. Occasionally, one of them is brave enough to pull off a caper alone, but most of the time they work in pairs or threesomes. Some of their stings include the part-timer, Y, who is in a witness protection program and tends to disguise himself as an E or I. Don't ask me why.

A is considered a sacred vowel among pirates, who are known to be an irritable lot themselves. The question naturally arises were they just born irritable, or did the words "Aye" and "Arrg" turn these mild-mannered sailors into dangerous, cut-throat villains?

And what's up with that schwa sound? Is that someone's idea of a cruel joke? Who gave A the right to transform itself into an upside-down, lowercase E? This is one vowel who has read too many of its own press clippings.

Speaking of vowels on a head trip, E is the first letter in egomaniac. This goes back to the days of handset type when the largest compartment in the type case was reserved for the lowercase e. People incorrectly assumed that e earned this position by being the most frequently used letter in the alphabet. Not so. The lower case e is a bully who believes the entire universe revolves around him. Like Napoleon, he suffers from "little man" syndrome and forced four or five skinny consonants to give up their space to expand his empire.

The E also likes to flip-flop with I, especially when C is around. I know this sounds kinky, but hey, that's what vowels do. A funny thing about their little tryst with C is they set rules as to who goes first and then create a dozen exceptions to their own rule – reminds me of our politicians.

Now, let's examine the letter I. You may recognize this vowel from its appearance in the acronym for Ship High In Transit. When used in this manner, I has the ability to stretch itself into a slithering, three-syllable scream followed by an angry exclamation point. You may have heard your father use this acronym as an expletive after throwing a gutter ball or striking his thumb with a hammer. This word is very flexible and can also be used with prefixes such as "holy" or suffixes like "fire."

I has earned the reputation as the most self-centered and irritable of all vowels. It can be used in conjunction with consonants or other vowels, but prefers to stand alone. You can't read an essay or first person novel without I hogging center stage and acting like a know-it-all. It's I this and I that all the way through the story. Let's face it, I is an exhibitionist who can't get enough of seeing its own slender figure in print.

What about O, you ask? How much trouble can a big, round circle cause? Plenty. O will lull you into a sense of false security and then jump up and bite you in the orifice when you least expect it. While other vowels may publicly flaunt their self-importance, O humbly considers itself the omnipotent authority of the alphabet. If O wants your opinion, it will tell you what it is.

Lowercase Os are like teenagers. They tend to run in pairs. They start out playing nice as in wool, look, or maroon. Then, when no one's expecting it, they jump up and yell, "BOOB!" Even after the laughter dies it takes two weeks to wipe the smiles off their faces.

If there's one letter in the alphabet that has more psychological issues than a Tasmanian Devil on Prozac, it's U. The reason? The problem is never me – it's always U. See what I mean?

U's low self-esteem stems from the fact it has been teased for centuries about being an upside down, lower case n. Nothing could be further from the truth, but after being used twice in the spelling of Uranus (not to mention the phrase "your anus") this vowel is highly sensitive and easily upset. Be careful how you use it. Things can get ugly real quick.

Now that you've been armed with the facts about Irritable Vowel Syndrome, I hope that you'll choose your letters carefully before spelling your next word. The same holds true in conversations, especially with your boss, spouse, or a priest during confessional.

There are a lot of words out there that can get you into trouble and every single one of them contains at least one vowel. Use discretion when sprinkling them throughout a sentence. Who knows, you may be forced to eat them later.

Young Dr. Jung
or
Samurai Vasectomy

The nurse ordered me to remove my pants and underwear. I stared down at my freshly shaved family jewels and wondered if they'd still love me in the morning. There was a weak knock on the door and a young woman entered the room.

"Hello, I'm Dr. Jung."

My jaw hit the floor.

The receptionist who called the day before said *Dr. Young* would be performing the procedure. I imagined Dr. Young to be a distinguished gentleman in his mid-forties with a hint of gray in his temples like one of those guys in the "Just for Men" commercials.

The person who stood before me was a petite, twenty-something, Asian girl.

Sirens screamed, and flashing red lights illuminated the inner recesses of my brain. The movie theater inside my head skipped the previews and cut straight to the hospital scene in the movie *Stir Crazy*. An inmate who had been castrated leans over to Richard Pryor and says, "They got this Korean doctor who just set foot in this country. Make sure you don't get him. He's the one who made the mistake on me."

"Are you Mr. Gayer?" she said, with only a slight accent.

I wanted to ask her if she was from Korea, but didn't have the balls. It was an awkward moment for both of us. Before I could respond there was another knock. A man old enough to be my father entered the room.

"Hi, I'm Dr. Patrick. I'll be assisting Dr. Jung."

A couple of loose wires between my ears connected for a tenth of a second.

It was an, "Oh, Shit!" moment.

Dr. Jung would be taking her first stab at Neutering 101 with my scrotum portraying Most Terrified Supporting Actor in a documentary. She gave me a weak smile and tried to put on a mask of confidence. It didn't fit well and kept sliding to one side. She straightened it up a couple of times, like she was embarrassed, then finally just took it off.

Sterilization is not something a man takes lightly. We don't run around waving a flag and hollering, "Hurry, somebody neuter me. I've got no business fathering children."

Nope, a decision of this magnitude requires some heavy thinking and powerful persuasion. Fortunately, I'm married to someone who's pretty good at both.

My original plan to have enough kids to field a ball team hit a brick wall. Our second child was born with an infection in his lungs and spent eight days in intensive care. The doctor said a rare form of bacteria inside the mother was the cause. Any future pregnancies would run the same risk. My wife and I debated it briefly and decided two kids would be enough.

Over the next year and a half, we had several serious discussions about birth control. We were still in our twenties and my wife didn't want to be on the pill for two more decades. Creams, foams, condoms, and other options were messy and definite mood killers. Centuries old tactics, such as the rhythm method, were quickly eliminated. Neither of us could keep up with dates on a calendar, and since I wasn't coordinated enough to clap my hands in time with music, how could she expect me to provide rhythm during sex? That left only one alternative – surgery.

One of us would have to go under the knife.

The odds are stacked against the male of the species when it comes to making a decision about who will be sterilized.

Sure, vasectomies are cheaper, less invasive, and have a faster recovery time, but so what? This is manhood we're talking about. The combination of poor self esteem and mental anguish should be enough to justify a legitimate defense for protecting one's scrotum.

"There is one other option we haven't considered," said my wife.

"What's that?"

"Celibacy"

Three days later I found myself at the Planned Parenthood office of the Washington County Human Services Department. A more accurate name would be the Plan-Not-To-Be-A-Parent Office of Human Neutering Services. The young lady behind the desk had a most cheerful conversation with my wife while I signed hundreds of documents authorizing them to cut holes in me and do whatever they deemed necessary to keep my seed from further populating the earth. She handed me a little brochure explaining the procedure and scheduled the surgery thirty days out. This would give me an opportunity to back out should my feet turn to icebergs.

In the weeks leading up to my surgery, everyone in our circle of friends offered words of encouragement and support. The women all patted me on the back and commended me for being such a "real man" who would do the "right thing" for his wife. The men, most of whom would rather commit suicide than have a vasectomy, offered comforting words like, "It's no big deal. You'll be over it in no time. And – my Uncle Billy got an infection and they had to cut his nuts off!"

I had that last comment stuffed in File 13 until Dr. Jung introduced herself.

Under normal situations I would have considered her an attractive young woman, but based upon what was scheduled to occur, she looked more like the Bride of Frankenstein than a practicing physician.

The elder doctor began describing the vasectomy game plan in minute detail to Dr. Jung while she drenched my genitals in betadine solution, coating me from navel to my knees.

When comparing notes a few years later, a friend related that a beautiful blonde nurse assisted with the prep work and he became so aroused they had to restrain his member. Let me assure you, that did NOT happen with me!

"Your scrotum sure is drawn up," said Dr. Patrick. I don't know what he expected. They had me laid out on a slab of frozen granite in a sub-zero examining room.

"Yours would be too if someone was coming at it with a knife," I replied.

He ignored my response and quickly changed the subject. We got into a short conversation about his daughter. She and I were in the same class in first grade. Twenty-four years later she was living the good life in Greece, while I was baring my genitals to a rookie doctor. Maybe it is *not* such a small world after all.

"I'm going to give you a local to numb the area." Dr. Patrick held a syringe up toward the light, squinted one eye, and flicked it a couple of times with this middle finger. Satisfied the air bubbles were released into the atmosphere, he began injecting my nether regions as if he were marinating a Thanksgiving turkey. By the time he was done perforating the pin cushion of my manhood, tears were streaming down my cheeks, and my knuckles were white from crushing handfuls of the granite table into a fine, powdery sand.

Normally, when a doctor gives you a shot of novocaine, he leaves the room for a few minutes to shoot the breeze with a pharmaceutical salesman while the medication kicks in.

Not Dr. Patrick.

He immediately began demonstrating to Dr. Jung how to locate and identify the tiny tubes that served as the pipelines of propagation. Rolling the left-side tube between his finger and thumb he worked it into position, as close to the surface of the skin as possible. Then grabbing a set of C-shaped forceps from his little tool chest, he encircled the tube and clicked the locking mechanism down to the seventh notch, crushing my tender flesh in a stainless steel vise.

"Yeoow!" My pelvic area shot skyward, and my eyes sprang from their sockets like a cartoon character grabbing a bare electrical wire.

"Hmmm, that local must not be working," said Dr. Patrick. "Do you need another shot?"

"No!" I screamed between gasps for breath. "It's only been thirty seconds. Let's give the first one a chance to work." He tilted his head and scrunched his brow as if I was speaking in a foreign language, then picked up a scalpel and showed it to Dr. Jung.

"We make an incision right here," he said. A thin trail of blood chased the blade across my sacrificial groin. My stomach churned like a washing machine. I couldn't stand to watch, yet couldn't look away.

"Then we pull out the tube."

He inserted an instrument resembling a crochet hook into the opening and extracted an angel-hair-spaghetti-size-strand from my quivering scrotum. Pulling a spool of black fishing line from his tackle box, he tied off both ends and clipped out the section between the knots. After a lengthy dissertation to Dr. Jung, he stuffed the loose ends back into the hole, closed the incision with two stitches, and removed the clamp.

"Now, you do the other side," he said.

I made eye contact with Dr. Jung. She swallowed hard. Her hands were shaking like a Chihuahua battling Parkinson's. The thought of handing this woman a knife and telling her to "go for it" made my testicles want to crawl up in my belly and hide behind the bright yellow organ known as my liver. I could visualize my family jewels being reduced to a single pearl dangling from a gossamer thread.

She exhaled deeply and began following Dr. Patrick's instructions as he led her step-by-step through the procedure. By now, I was numb from the chin down and didn't flinch when she tightened the forceps. That must've given her confidence for her shaking faded to a mere tremble. She managed to complete the job, leaving the remainder my organs intact except for the small section of tube, which I'm sure she kept as a souvenir of her initiation into the Neutering Club of American Physicians.

I limped back to the waiting room where my wife was grinning from ear to ear. That night, I kept my feet up and wore an icepack on the affected area until bedtime. After a couple of days of impersonating a bow-legged cowboy, I was able to resume normal activities.

If you're a male considering a vasectomy, let me assure you, *you will not be less of a man.* The physical pain is minimal and short lived (unless of course your name is Uncle Billy), and the mental anguish only lasts two or three decades.

When it comes to selecting a doctor, don't be afraid to choose a young female from Korea. They are kind, gentle, and compassionate. It's the guy old enough to be your dad – who has obviously lost all feeling in his own groin – that you need to stay away from.

Outdoor Misadventures

People born and raised in the South run a high risk of exposure to wildlife. Sometimes this even involves contact with woodland creatures or fish. Many times I've been challenged to battle wits with these wild beasts in their natural habitat. This puts me at a severe disadvantage since they are using all their wits and I only have half of mine. Evidently, I inherited my "wildlife skills" from my dad and uncles, who had their own struggles mastering the great outdoors.

Lost at Peter Bottom

The trail disappeared.

In my limited experience as a six year old boy, I had never seen a trail in Northwest Arkansas, or anywhere else for that matter, just up and disappear – *and without a trace*!

One minute I was plodding along in complete confidence that the route to my destination would be as swift and trouble-free as devouring one of the homemade fried pies my mother had packed for our lunch when, from out of nowhere – and without the slightest forewarning – the darn thing just evaporated. Even worse, the path behind me took notice and decided to join his evil twin by participating in this cruel prank.

Realizing that I was sorely misplaced, and my sense of direction in severe need of an extensive overhaul, I did the only logical thing. I panicked.

Words for my epitaph played on the phonograph inside my brain. *Boy of six. Lost at Peter Bottom on War Eagle River. His body never found.*

How the relatives would cry and carry on.

"He was such a sweet boy," the old women from church would say.

"That boy loved to play baseball. Might have made it to the majors too," the kindly old gentleman down the road would remark.

The sun bore down with profound intensity from its position directly overhead. Mr. Solar Power could have helped me if he wanted to, by sliding to the east or west, or at least providing a shadow by which I might gain some great and powerful revelation of divine nature.

But no. He chose to remain motionless, even convincing the wind to cease, as to render the impression that time had indeed stood still.

The scenery looked the same in every direction. Ragweeds and river cane soared into the air. Their towering stalks crowded into an immense jungle at least two hundred feet tall. The wind returned as a gentle breeze, slithering its way through the weeds to create an evil hiss. Hair stood on the back of my neck, goose bumps raced down my arms, and a lump the size of pumpkin took up residence inside my throat.

River bottoms are notorious for snakes. Vicious Copperheads, loathsome Water Moccasins, an occasional Rattler, and the ever-bloodthirsty Cottonmouth were all known to call this stretch of bottom land home. And, rumor was, they weren't crazy about strangers.

I began to question the wisdom of leaving Uncle Harry on the comfortable stretch of gravel bar below the shoal all alone. It was peaceful there. Hundred-year-old trees rose stately from the river bank. Their magnificent canopies cast a cool and welcome shade on the bleach-white gravels. There were rocks to skip and mussel shells to scoop sand from the water's edge. Why did I ever leave the safety and security of such an oasis?

The answer is simple. Greed.

This was a fishing trip. The primary goal when fishing is to catch fish. We had worked this hole quite a while with no success. I tried various types of bait, often leaving them in the same spot for an eternity of two whole minutes without getting so much as a nibble. Frustration mounted with each passing moment and the length of my patience could be measured against the point of a hook – with plenty of room to spare.

The waiting game didn't seem to bother Uncle Harry. When the going got slow, he would pull a tin of Velvet from his overall bibs and roll a cigarette. Each time he started this process, a fish close to the surface would relay a message to another at the end of the line to give the bait a couple of quick jerks. This would throw Uncle Harry into a temporary quandary, not knowing whether to pour the tobacco back into the tin or finish the cigarette. By the time he'd come to a decision and picked up the rod, the jerking would cease. Tiny bubbles popped to the surface near his line, evidence that the fish were having quite a chuckle at poor Harry's expense.

My father had taken up position about a hundred yards downriver. We could easily see him sitting on the edge of a mud bank with his rods propped in forked sticks. The roar of water tumbling down the rocky shoal made it difficult to communicate, fed to permission to leave the gravel bar and traverse the short distance from one outpost to the other.

I presumed this would be an easy task. After all, I had been on several such expeditions with my dad and Uncle Harry and was a seasoned veteran at following riverbank trails.

Or so I thought.

Now, I found myself in an endless jungle surrounded by thousands of snakes and several hundred unscrupulous wild beasts, all ready to sink their teeth into my tender young flesh. It was time to call upon the survival knowledge I had accumulated during my six short years and which I had often put to the test in such dire circumstances.

"Daddy!" I screamed. "Where are you?"

"Over here." It was hard to get a bearing on his muffled reply above the thrashing of canes and crush of leaves beneath my small, rapidly churning feet.

First, I darted one direction. Then stopped to holler again.

Now, the sound of Dad's voice was coming from a different place. Had he moved?

Charging forth another ten yards, I repeated the procedure. This went on for some time with both of us hollering back and forth, and me finally gathering sufficient horse sense to remain quiet long enough to gain a bead on his location.

My throat was dry and hoarse by the time a thin spot appeared in the canes. From this vantage point, I could see a bluff on the far bank and knew I was approaching the river's edge.

Two steps ahead lay the trail. Why it chose to magically reappear is unbeknownst to me. Perhaps it was tired of our little game, or maybe the screaming and crying had begun to wear on its nerves. In either case, it spat me out atop the bank near my father.

Dad welcomed me with open arms, and after a brief, but painless lecture, reached into his old canvas fishing bag and rewarded me with the tastiest fried pie that ever slid between a set of teeth and gums.

What a glorious homecoming that was! It reminds me of a passage of scripture. "My son was lost, but now is found. Let us kill the fatted pie and rejoice."

The One That Got Away

Pug finished the morning milking and was headed back to the house when he heard a car rumbling up the dusty gravel road. Looking over his shoulder, he saw Harry's faded blue 1950 Ford pass the log barn and turn into the driveway. Harry pulled up beside the shop and shut off the motor.

"Got your chores done?" Harry asked in the hoarse, raspy voice that had become his trademark.

"Yep, just finished" answered Pug. "I still need to go to the pond and get the minnows. Should we stop at Choc's house and see if he wants to go?"

"Good idea," said Harry. "It would be handy to have someone to paddle us from stump to stump and string our fish." Harry wiggled a thumb and forefinger into his overall bibs, fished out a red tin of Velvet tobacco, and began rolling a cigarette. "Want me to go the pond and get the minnows while you're getting your tackle ready?"

"Yeah, that'd be a big help. I'll get my stuff and back the truck up to the boat. When you get back, we'll load up and go see what Choc is doing."

With the accuracy and precision of tag-team wrestlers, the brothers-in-law shoved the boat into the back of the pick-up and headed down the road. At the top of the hill, they turned into a long, catalpa-lined driveway that ended in Choc's front yard. There he stood, arms folded, pipe clenched firmly in his jaw, leaning against the back of his old pink and white Oldsmobile.

"Where you fellers think you're headed?" Choc mumbled, his speech impaired by clamping his teeth together around the pipe stem that rarely left his mouth. The result was a unique enunciation of what had formerly been known as the English language.

"We're going to Pinhook to catch crappie and we need somebody to string fish for us. Wanna go?" Pug asked.

"Sounds like fun," snorted Choc. "But you'll have to string your own dang fish. In fact, I'll probably keep you boys busy stringing mine." He flipped open his Zippo and relit his pipe for the third time in five drags.

He lifted his rod and reel from the sixteen-penny nail on the garage wall and deposited it in the boat with the rest of the tackle. Pug fired up the old pick-up and they headed to the bend in the White River known as Pinhook.

The U.S. Army Corps of Engineers completed construction on the Beaver Lake dam in 1966. As a result, rising lake water engulfed the standing timber at the mouth of Mill Hollow where a tiny feeder creek poured into the river. Their boyhood swimming hole was now submerged, but the flooded timber had become a haven for bass, bream, catfish, and especially crappie.

Backing up to shoreline, they eased the flat-bottom boat into the water. Choc was assigned the back seat of the boat, Harry took the middle and Pug sat in the bow.

"Paddle me out to that big cedar, Choc" said Harry, as he rolled another cigarette. "There's a big 'un out there with my name on it." Choc grumbled something inaudible and steered the aluminum craft toward the sprawling cedar.

"Cut it hard to the right," ordered Pug. "We don't want to ram the brush pile. It might scare the fish away." Choc bit harder into his pipe stem and mumbled another series of choice expletives. They tied off the ends of the boat, baited up, and weaved their minnows through the tangled web of tree limbs. Harry's bobber disappeared below the surface as soon as it hit the water. He set the hook, gracefully guided his speckled prize over the outstretched branches and tossed it at Choc's feet.

"There's the first one!" Harry threw out his chest and crowed like a rooster at daybreak. Over the next fifteen minutes, he deposited half a dozen more around Choc's ankles. By then, Pug had caught four while Choc's bobber continued to sit motionless amidst the cedar branches.

"Choc, if you ain't gonna help us catch these things the least you could do is put 'em on a stringer," said Pug. He spat a long, brown stream of tobacco juice across the water to add an exclamation point. Choc lowered his head and glared at his brother over the top of his horned-rimmed glasses. Steam poured from his ears.

"I told you boys you were gonna have to string your own goll-darn fish, cause I'm about to catch the whopper of the day." The words had not cleared the thin gap between his lips and pipe stem when his bobber began to jiggle.

"Choc, you're getting a bite" said Harry. The red and white plastic globe skittered toward the heavy timber, then dove like a submarine.

"Pull up on him," said Pug. "Don't let him get in that thick brush."

Choc ground his teeth into the pipe stem and gave the pole a quick jerk. The tip of his fiberglass rod curled downward, chasing the line into the water. The fish charged to the left, to the right, toward the boat, then away from it. Choc jammed the rod handle to his belly, leaned back, and cranked the reel like a madman. For every foot of line he'd gain the fish would take two. The drag on the reel was squealing like a spoiled brat in a candy store. He worked the fish off one entanglement, only to find another. Choc rose to his feet and jerked the rod up and down in hopes of dislodging his fish from the brush pile.

"Try giving it some slack, then pull the fish back up to the hang," said Pug. "Sometimes they'll swim around the limb."

Choc followed his brother's instructions and, to his relief, it worked. When the green monster appeared on the surface, Choc's eyes ballooned to the size baseballs and his jaw fell open for the first time since breakfast, pipe teetering from his lower lip. Harry and Pug later testified that the fish would've measured twenty inches long and four inches thick on an official Fisherman's De-Liar measuring tape.

"Get the net! Get the net! Get the net!" Choc screamed.

Harry dug through the flopping fish in the floor of the boat and grabbed the hoop of the net. He tried to lift it, but something was holding it down.

"You're standing on the handle." He yelled at Choc.

Choc raised his left foot, assuming a flamingo-style pose. Without warning, advance notice, or the least bit of common consideration, the lunker made a mad dash for open water. It shot like a torpedo around the back of the boat, twisting Choc into a pretzel and wrapping the rod around his neck. In less time than a fast talking preacher could say, "In the name of the Father," Choc received his baptism.

He landed flat on his back and sank like an anvil. Thrashing and kicking, he popped to the surface. Water poured off the bill of his cap and into the bowl of his pipe, still cemented firmly between clenched teeth.

"I'll give that dive a 9.8 for technical merit," said Harry, "but only 3.5 for style."

"I score it 8.6 overall, but he gets extra credit for the level of difficulty," said Pug.

"Ha ha," sputtered Choc, "very funny. Now that you've had your laugh, help me back in the boat." Harry clasped Choc's forearm and pulled him belly-first over the end of the boat. Choc unlaced his shoes and poured out the water while Pug and Harry paddled to shore.

Halfway through loading the boat Choc's eyes bugged out again. He dropped his end of the flat bottom and began kicking both legs high in the air and shaking the front of his overalls.

"This ain't no time for dancing, Choc. Heck, there ain't even no music playing." Pug laughed.

"By God, there is something in my overalls besides me!" yelled Choc. He continued the Irish folkdance until the object of his distress shot out the bottom of his pants leg. Pug reached down and picked up a three-inch perch at Choc's feet.

"Look at the bright side, Choc," said Harry. "At least you didn't get skunked!"

Sack of Suckers

"When the dogwoods are in full bloom the suckers are on the shoal." That's what the old timers used to say. Snagging (or grabbing, in hillbilly vernacular) has been an Ozark tradition for generations. The fish were cleaned, chopped, stuffed into jars, and canned using a pressure cooker. Patties, or 'fishcakes', were made by adding egg and a little flour to the canned fish and frying in a cast iron skillet. Sadly, man-made lakes and lack of access to prime spawning locations have made grabbing a thing of the past. Only a few old timers remain, and their number dwindles each year. This is my attempt to capture the essence of that tradition and honor those who loved it.

It was about nine o'clock when Pug's old Chevy pick-up popped over the crest and onto the floor of the War Eagle Mill Bridge. The heavy wooden timbers made a cloppity-clop noise under the tires as the truck crept slowly toward the center of the bridge.

Billy Stafford was draped over the iron rail, slinging his hooks upriver and jerking them back down. Four or five fish tails were sticking out of the top of his five gallon bucket.

"'Bout to get a bucket full, Billy?" Pug asked as he rolled to a stop.

"Well, there's a few in there," said Billy as looked over his shoulder. "Who's that you're hauling around with you today?"

he snorted, gazing at Choc and Harry. "You know these yellow suckers don't like the smell of pipe smoke. I believe I'd left that old codger at home."

"I think you got that backwards, Billy," mumbled Choc.

He always spoke with his teeth clamped together whether the pipe was in his mouth or not. The result was a unique presentation of what had formerly been known as the English language.

"When they smell this pipe smoke they come swimming up the river like piss ants to honey. Then all I got to do is have Pug to take 'em off my hooks and get Rip to sack 'em up."

"One thing for sure," said Harry, in the hoarse, raspy voice that had become his trademark. "There's never a dull moment when you're fishing with Choc."

"It takes two people just to see after him," he chuckled, stuffing his Velvet tobacco tin back in his overall bibs after rolling a cigarette,

"Well, we better get off the bridge before a car comes," said Pug. He eased his foot off the clutch and guided the old truck down into the dirt parking area across from the mill.

They crawled out of the cab, untied their cane poles and headed down to the gravel bar. It had rained a little the night before. The river hadn't come up much, but the water had a good dingy color. There was a good current, but not too strong. Conditions were just right to entice suckers into migrating up river for their annual spawning ritual.

Pug had made several sets of grabs the night before, each consisting of nine single hooks about five inches apart. He had neatly wrapped them around a large piece of Styrofoam for tangle-free transportation. This also minimized downtime when a new set was required after hanging up and breaking off.

They each tied on a set of grabs, adding sinkers above and below the hooks to keep them close to the bottom as they traveled down stream over the rough gravels.

Choc waded in almost to his knees. "Water's pretty chilly," he reported.

Slowly he swung his long cane pole up river, depositing his hooks as far up stream as possible. About halfway through the first drag Choc felt something hit his hooks and gave a quick jerk. Moments later he wrestled a two pound sucker onto the gravel bar.

"There's the first one!" he crowed.

It wasn't long before both Harry and Pug were pulling in fish too. Pretty soon the three of them had eight or ten yellow suckers and a couple of red horse lying on the rocky shore.

"Guess we ought to sack these," said Harry, dragging another fish to the bank. "Don't want 'em to start drying out." He reached into Pug's old canvas hunting bag and pulled out three burlap feed sacks.

"That's a good idea," said Choc, cane pole bouncing from the weight of his latest catch. "You sack 'em, Rip. Me and Pug will keep you busy."

Harry distributed the fish in the three sacks and placed a large rock on the neck of each to keep them from drifting away in the current. Then he sat down and rolled another cigarette. By the time he had it finished and lit two more suckers had landed at his feet.

Within a couple of hours the three anglers had totaled thirty-five to forty fish and the action had begun to slow down.

Pug and Harry waded out of the water and sat down on the gravel bar to rest. "Got some good fried apple pies here if you're hungry, Choc," said Pug.

"I'll be out in a minute," answered Choc, continuing to swing his pole up river. Suddenly he felt a hard thump against his line. The end of his sixteen-foot pole bucked violently. Z-z-z-i-ippp his line sang, shooting up river.

"Got a big 'un on!" he hollered, fighting to maintain control of the cane pole.

Choc staggered forward a few feet, attempting to improve his leverage on the wild beast at the end of his line. Without warning the line went slack, quickly followed by an emerald flash as the huge red horse darted downstream and behind him. In less than a heartbeat the fish had encircled his knees and made a mad dash for deeper water.

The line jerked taunt, yanking Choc's knees together. For a brief second he tottered like an inverted pyramid, arms flailing in a vain attempt to keep his balance.

Ker-splash! He disappeared beneath the rolling current.

The next thing Pug and Harry saw was Choc's wide brimmed straw hat floating down stream. Choc clambered to his feet, pipe still clenched firmly between his teeth, and watched in dismay as the large red horse surfaced in front of him, waving its crimson tail as if to say goodbye.

"Looks like the big 'un got you," chided Harry, between bellows of laughter. "Minnie's gonna wonder why you didn't wait until you got home to take a bath."

"Want me to get you a bar of soap, Choc?" laughed Pug.

Choc mumbled and grumbled some unpleasantries as he sloshed ashore, pulled his billfold and tobacco pouch from his overalls and lay them on the ground to dry in the warm April sun.

Pug retrieved Choc's hat and after a few more merciless jokes about baptism by red horse, he and Harry picked up their poles and started fishing again.

About his second or third cast Harry pulled out a nice sucker. He untangled his hooks from the fish and tossed it on the gravel bar. "Hey Choc, while you're sitting there sun-bathing why don't you sack that fish for me?"

"It would be my pleasure," said Choc, with a gleam of mischief in his eyes.

By now, it was late afternoon and all three sacks were heavy with fish. "Boys, we're gonna have to quit after a few more drags," warned Pug. "My old cows are gonna be waiting at the milk barn."

"Well, I'm ready any time you are," said Harry. They waded ashore, secured their grabs to the cane poles with electrical tape, and gathered the remainder of their tackle.

"Rip, why don't you carry the poles and rest of the stuff," suggested Choc. "Me and Pug can carry these sacks of fish to the truck?"

"That suits me," answered Harry. "It's always nice to have somebody tote your fish."

Choc watched Harry scoop up the tackle and head down the trail. "Let's pull one on Ol' Rip," Choc whispered to Pug.

"What ya got in mind?"

"Let's take Rip's sack of fish and dump 'em back in the river, then fill the sack with rocks."

"Big brother, you are ornery and lowdown. Let's do it."

Harry was leaning against the side of the pick-up rolling another cigarette when Choc and Pug arrived with the sacks of fish. "It sure took you boys long enough," he said as he lit his smoke. "Thought I was gonna have to send out a search party to look for you."

"Your darned old fish are awful heavy," snorted Choc. He and Pug gently lowered the burlap sacks into the bed of the truck to avoid giving away the rocky contents to their unsuspecting brother in-law.

All the way home Harry continued to perfect his version of Choc's bath in the river. Most of the actual facts flew out the window. Minnie was going to hear how a six-inch river chub had almost drowned her husband.

Choc just sat in the middle of the bench seat smoking his pipe and occasionally nodding in agreement. From time to time he would look at Pug and give a little wink. "You're right, Rip," he agreed. "There *will* be a good story to tell."

Before long they pulled up in the yard at Choc's house. He and Harry quickly unloaded their tackle and poles and Choc drug out his sack of fish. "I believe that sack is yours, Rip. It was a lot heavier than mine or Pug's"

"That's what happens when you catch the most fish," Harry stated proudly. "I told you boys this morning that I was going to catch a whole sack of suckers."

"Well, dump it out on the ground and let's see how many you got," urged Pug.

Harry's sack hit the ground with a thud. Grasping the bottom of the sack and heaving upward he dumped half a wash tub of rocks out at his feet.

Harry stared down in disbelief, cigarette dangling from his lower lip.

"Well, Rip," said Choc, grinning from ear to ear, "who's the sucker now?"

The Carp Tournament

Pug pulled a large mixing bowl from the top shelf of the cabinet, poured it three-quarters full of Wheaties, and began crushing them with his hands. After mixing a handful of flour into the ground cereal, he took the dipper from the water bucket, drizzled a tiny stream over the mixture, and worked it into a dough.

It was still a little dry. *Good*, just enough room for the secret ingredient. He opened a bottle of Nehi Strawberry soda from the refrigerator and poured a few splashes over the dough, kneading it in. Rolling the cereal mix into a large ball he wrapped the homemade fish bait in wax paper and stuffed it in the old canvas hunting sack that doubled for a tackle box during the summer. Slinging the strap over his shoulder, he headed to the shop to gather up his fishing poles.

The screen door had barely slammed behind him when he heard a car rumbling down the gravel road. Harry' s old blue '50 Ford passed the log barn and pulled into the driveway. He shut off the motor and began fishing a red tin of Velvet tobacco from his overall bibs.

"Well, the weather looks favorable, Pug," he said, in his coarse, raspy voice. "You oughta get your pole bent today."

"I hope so," said Pug. "I made a good-sized dough ball. It ought to last all day unless Choc decides to feed on it too. And, I got a few milkworms in a lard bucket as a back-up in case we run out."

Harry opened the trunk and Pug loaded his fishing rods, hunting sack, and bucket of worms. When they arrived at

Choc's house they found him standing by the garage door with an old yellow housecat making figure eights between his feet. Harry got out of the car and began to roll another cigarette.

"'Bout ready for the big carp tournament, Choc?" he asked, before licking and sealing the paper.

"Ready as I'm gonna get." Choc always spoke out of one side of his mouth due to the fact that his teeth were permanently clamped around the stem of a pipe.

"Well, load your poles, and let's go," said Pug. "The day ain't getting any younger and neither are you."

Ten minutes later they arrived at the old Habberton Bridge place. The county had torn down the iron truss and wood-floor structure a few years back, but there was a good place to park at the end of the road, just a few steps from the river.

The trio unloaded their gear and headed up stream to the slough below Walker's Bluff, a notoriously good carp hole this time of year. Pug stopped at a Sycamore bush on the way and cut some forked sticks to use as rod props.

Passing around the giant ball of dough, they each pinched off a couple of pieces and formed acorn-size balls around their hooks. The sweet aroma of strawberry Wheaties filled the air as baits went flying across the open water into the river.

Pug took a chew of tobacco, Harry rolled a cigarette, and Choc loaded his old pipe (that had to be re-lit after every other drag). They sat down on the gravels, anxious to see who would get the first bite.

"Here's the rules, boys," said Pug. "Every time one of us catches a fish the other two have to put a dime in the pot. At the end of the day the man with the most fish and the man with the biggest fish split the pot 50-50."

"Hope you guys brought a lot of dimes," mumbled Choc, as the end of his rod began to twitch. He lifted the pole from its rest and heaved back with a mighty jerk. "Get ready to feed the pot." His rod bent nearly in half by the surging of his orange-lipped prey.

Before he could get it to the bank Harry had hooked one. A few minutes later Pug got in on the fun too. Within a couple of hours they had landed a total of 25 fish. Harry was in the lead with 10, followed by Pug with eight, and Choc close behind at seven.

"We've got enough bait for one more round," said Pug as he rolled the remainder of the dough into three balls. "So far all the carp are about the same size. No clear cut winner on the biggest fish, but that's fixin' to change." Working up a mouthful of tobacco juice he grabbed his line between the hook and sinker and spat a brown stream of "good luck" juice on his bait, coating the entire dough ball with a dark slime.

With a smooth swing of his right arm he gracefully cast the tobacco-drenched bait midway of the river. When the sinker hit bottom, he rolled up the slack and leaned the rod against the forked stick. His butt hadn't even settled on the gravels when a couple of quick tugs indicated a fish had found the bait. Pug lifted the rod and waited for the line to pull taut, then with a quick, hard jerk, he set the hook.

"I put the steel into that one," he bellowed. The fiberglass pole bent into a U-shape and the battle was on. For the first twenty minutes the carp took control. She swam up and down the river at will, forcing the drag to squeal like tires on a teenager's hotrod. Yard after yard of line peeled from the reel as the fish fought valiantly for freedom.

In the meantime, Choc caught another medium sized fish and Harry rolled in his poles so that Pug's behemoth wouldn't get tangled in the lines.

"You gonna land that thing today, or should we come back and pick you up next week," said Choc.

"I think she's starting to wear down," said Pug. But as soon as the words left his lips the monster fish made another run. Every time he worked her close to the bank the fish would get a second wind and dart back to the deep. Over and over the cycle repeated with Choc and Harry casting bets on who would wear out first, Pug or the fish.

The battle continued for another forty-five minutes before fish finally appeared to give up the ghost. Totally exhausted, she lay on her side and allowed Pug to tow her into ankle deep water. The carp was at least three and a half feet in length, and even Choc agreed that she would weigh close to 60 pounds.

"Harry, get behind her and help me get her up on the gravel bar," pleaded a worn out Pug.

"No can do," said Harry. "It would be a violation of tournament rules. You can't touch another man's fish. You gotta land her yourself or it don't count."

Pug bent over the huge carp and slid his hand behind her gills. With one final surge of energy the fish gave a mighty flop. Like a bucking bronco, she threw an off-balanced Pug somersaulting into river.

While he lay flat on his back – dazed and confused – she slowly maneuvered around the outstretched angler and eased her way back into the channel. The hook had become dislodged when Pug was thrown through the air and lay shining on the sand at the water's edge.

After a hearty round of laughter and gymnastics jokes, Harry and Choc pulled Pug to his feet and back on dry land. He was sopping wet, but the only thing that appeared bruised was his ego.

"Well, Pug," said Harry, "you missed out on the money. But while Choc and I are splitting up the pot, you can sing us a couple verses of that old sad song. You know, it's one of your favorites – *The One That Got Away.*"

Redneck GPS

"Whatcha working on, Randy?" I asked, peeking curiously over his shoulder.

"GPS software." He replied in a low monotone drawl. My presence appeared to be more of an annoyance that a welcome visit from an old hunting buddy.

"What's new to invent with that? GPS has been around for years."

"I'm creating customized voice response applications, if you must know. Human beings don't talk with that staccato delivery that most programs use. So, it occurred to me that there must be a huge untapped market for ethnic and regional voice response models. You know, like an Amish version that would say, 'Thou must turn right at the end of this section,' or one for inner-city blacks that would respond to a missed turn with, 'You missed the damn road, fool! Now, I's got to recalculate da freakin' route.'"

"Well, I've got to admit, that's an interesting approach. But what about guys like me?"

"Don't worry, buddy. I've got you covered. It's called Redneck Road Hunter."

"Redneck Road Hunter?" I chuckled. "How do you plan to market that?"

"Shouldn't be too hard. All I have to do is get Foxworthy or Larry the Cable Guy to endorse it and it'll sell millions. There will be regional packages for south Alabama, Mississippi, Arkansas, and of course the Midwest states like Nebraska will want theirs too. This country is full of rednecks, a huge untapped market," he said.

"But isn't road hunting unethical and illegal? Are you actually going to *help* people break the law?"

"Oh, no. Not at all. I'm just providing a tool. It's no different than those shops that sell water pipes and rolling papers for smoking dope. The stand-alone product breaks no law in itself. The consumer decides how they use it."

"Well, I can just see PETA picketing your house, along with all those other groups that advocate ethical hunting and animal rights."

"I'm not too worried about that. After the product has been on the market a couple of months I'll be living on a thousand-acre fenced reserve in Montana with armed guards at the gate. Let 'em picket till their butt cheeks freeze off. I don't care."

"Have you tested this Redneck Road Hunter yet? How do you know it's gonna work?"

Randy spun around in his chair. "Why do you think I called you?" He grinned. "Every product has to have a test pilot. Today's your lucky day! The first man in America to invoke the aid of Redneck Road Hunter in pursuit of the ever elusive white-tailed deer. You should feel extremely honored."

"Whoa, Nelly," I threw my hands up and took a couple of steps back. "I'm not so sure I want to get involved with road testing thing. Me and the game warden are on pretty good terms, and I'd like to keep it that way."

"We're not going to take a gun, you dummy. We'll just drive around out in the sticks for a couple of hours and test the voice response. I'm not asking you to do anything illegal."

It was apparent that Randy wasn't going to take "No" for an answer, and I'll have to admit curiosity was eating me alive.

"We'll take my truck," he offered, "but you'll have to drive. I've already got the software for Madison County loaded. There are a thousand dirt roads out there that neither of us have ever been on. The perfect place to test a prototype."

Half an hour later we turned off the pavement onto a narrow graveled road. "Hope you've got enough gas," I grumbled. "I'd hate to get lost and meet up with some of those guys from *'Deliverance'* out here."

"We can't get lost," snapped Randy, obviously irritated by my lack of faith. "We've got GPS, you idiot!"

He leaned over and activated the power button on the GPS. Within a couple of minutes the instrument identified our exact coordinates and a small map appeared on the screen.

"How y'all are?" a friendly male voice beckoned from the speaker. Immediately images of an overweight country boy with missing teeth, tobacco stains on his chin, and wearing a camouflage ball cap flashed into my mind. "We got some real good deer country coming up in the next two miles," the voice continued, "Ya need to turn right by that old log barn at the Y."

"Sounds pretty redneck," I observed. "Does it measure in yards and miles too?"

"Neither," Randy grinned from ear to ear. "I turned that function off. It recognizes landmarks from satellite images like those you see when you Google your house, along with topo-graphical information to guide you to the best possible deer-sighting opportunities. The only time it responds in miles is when you are searching for the nearest gas station or liquor store."

We turned right at the old barn and herded Randy's beat-up Chevy down an ever-narrowing path that resembled a cow trail more than a dirt road.

"Slow down!" barked the voice from the box. "There's a little clearing coming up on the left where the mailman's been seeing a big ten pointer."

"How does he know that?" I glared at Randy, skeptically.

"I've got my sources. Mailmen, school bus drivers, UPS guys, it's a network thing. The information is out there, you just have to know who to talk to and how to get it."

Sure enough, when we got to the clearing our eyes beheld one of the largest bucks on the face of the earth, standing broadside about forty yards off the road. He slowly raised his head, and turning our way displayed one of those huge rocking-chair racks you only see in hunting magazines or TV shows. Quickly perceiving that we were probably more foe than friend he bolted from the clearing, white flag waving goodbye through the scattered post oaks.

"Wow, that was cool." For a moment we sat in reverent silence. "How many points do you think he had?"

"At least twelve," guessed Randy. "Now, stop your droolin' and let's get movin'. Hey! That's a pretty good line." He laughed, tickled at his own rhyme. "Remind me to program that phrase into the voice responder library when we get back."

Shaking my head in utter disbelief at the depth to which he was amusing himself with redneck word-play, I stepped on the gas and resumed our course to parts unknown.

A few minutes later the silence was broken by the deep-woods drawl of our computerized companion. "The Cotter place is coming up on the right. There's usually deer in the persimmon patch around that rusty old Farmall."

Once again, there they were. Two does and three fawns causally fed on scattered sprigs of clover, as if patiently waiting for the fruit above to ripen and fall. After several minutes the matriarch of the group took a few steps forward to investigate the unusual visitors. She must have gotten a whiff of Randy's deodorant (or lack thereof), stamped her foot, snorted loudly, and led the rest of the quintet to the safety of a nearby thicket.

We hadn't gone far past the fallen-down homestead when Randy indicated he wanted to stop. "I need to stretch my legs and get a breath of this clean, country air," he announced, bouncing from the cab. Clearly there was more to his agenda than stretching and breathing, but correcting him would have gained nothing, so I slid from my seat to commune with nature as well.

Two minutes later we stopped again when it suddenly occurred to Randy that the persistent rattling in the tool box was a pair of binoculars he had brought along for visual aid. Before he could get the door fully open our country-fried companion started complaining. "You must have the bladder of a chipmunk. How many beers you had, for Christ's sake? I thought we come out here to look for deer, not to water the dandelions."

"Your creation is rather mouthy," I smirked. "Does he always talk to you like that?" Refusing to acknowledge my question, Randy quickly grabbed the binoculars climbed back into his seat.

Over the next two hours we must have traveled 25 to 30 miles of back roads. Past active farms and deserted homesteads, across low-water bridges, through deep forests, and alongside green briar patches so dense you couldn't see five feet back into the thicket.

Our redneck guide never led us astray. He knew the name on every mailbox before we got to them, and foretold purple paint and no trespassing signs with astounding accuracy. He even knew where the game wardens staked out the 'dummy deer', and warned us not to be fooled by the twitching tail or bobbing head. Overall, he was eight out of ten on deer-sighting predictions, and began to show more tolerance for frequent stops as the trip wore on.

Shortly after hitting the pavement Randy punched in *Liquor Store* on the menu and the shortest path quickly appeared on the screen.

"I've got to hand it to you, this GPS program is all you advertised and more," I raved. "It's amazing how much detailed data this thing contains and the accuracy rate on deer-sightings is absolutely unbelievable! Have you considered naming it? You know, like Hal the computer in *2001 A Space Odyssey?*"

"You know, I hadn't given it any thought until this afternoon. Then, it occurred to me while we were driving around that the obvious choice was to name it after the test pilot. I'm going to call him Delbert," deadpanned Randy. "Yep, Delbert the deer-finder, in honor of you."

"I don't know whether to be flattered or pissed off, but I guess it's not every day a person gets an electronic device named after them. This is going to take some getting used to."

"Yee-haw! It's beer-thirty," hollered Delbert, as we pulled up to the drive through.

"Wow, you boys are really excited. Had a long hard day?" asked the young lady at the window.

"Nah," said Randy. "That was our GPS. We've been out riding dirt roads, and he's been showing us deer."

"Oh, really?" replied our lovely attendant. "Maybe I shouldn't sell you boys any beer. Sounds like you've both had way too much already."

It took about ten minutes, but I was finally able to convince her that neither Randy nor I was intoxicated, and that my passenger was a bit of an eccentric who often tried to shock people by making up outrageous stories. After all, she would have never believed the truth. Finally she handed over the beer and we drove away.

We had barely got out of the parking lot and onto the highway when I heard the unmistakable sound of a beer top popping. "Whatcha got planned for next Saturday?" asked Randy, in between gulps of frosty brew. "Would you be interested in test piloting another prototype?"

"Sure, I had a great time today. Where are headed, Mississippi, Alabama, Missouri?

"Nah, none of those. I was thinking ..." Randy paused in mid-sentence for a deep guttural belch, "Harlem."

More Than One Way to Skin a Skunk

Six hundred dollars was a lot of money. That's how much Dad and my brother Gordon made on a week-long hunting and trapping expedition on the banks of the Mulberry River. They camped just east of Redding Park a few miles from Cass, Arkansas.

Daylight hours were spent scouting for sign, setting and baiting traps, and squeezing in a couple hours of sleep. After supper, Dad would light the kerosene lantern and they would spend half the night following the siren voice of Minnie Pearl, his blue-tick hound, up and down the steep, flint rock infested hillsides of the Ozark National Forest.

Inspired by their success, I took it upon myself to become the world's first millionaire trapper. If that didn't work out, I'd become the world's youngest thousand dollar a week trapper, and if that failed, an extra five to ten dollars would be a nice supplement to my two dollar a week salary for bucket feeding calves and caring for a house of chickens.

Dad had hunted and trapped since he was old enough to carry a rabbit gum. I'd followed him on several trap runs and figured I had enough expertise to become the next trapping legend of the Ozarks. Fur prices were at an all-time high and the harvest loomed ripe for the picking.

In preparation for my multi-million dollar venture, I grabbed a pole axe and began sharpening boards of various widths. The hundreds of pelts I was planning on taking would have to be turned inside out and stretched over V-shaped planks and hung to dry in the backroom of the old house.

The exact age of the old house never came up in polite conversation. We didn't ask and she didn't tell. For all I knew, she was constructed about the same time as the Great Pyramids of Giza. The building contained a stockpile of sacred relics including empty fruit jars, broken furniture and appliances, and a never-ending supply of things Mom couldn't bear to part with such as past issues of Progressive Farmer and Grit magazines. Should a band of ancient Egyptians happen along and need a place to store Pharaoh's sarcophagus, we had plenty of reading material to help get him through the afterlife.

Friday afternoon came and I was ready to put my plan in action. I hopped off the school bus and ran to the house to change clothes. There was two hours of daylight left, just enough time to set half a dozen traps before dark. Dad was cracking walnuts when I found him in the shop.

"I'd like to borrow some of your traps and catch some critters," I declared.

"And where to do you plan on catching these critters?" he asked.

"There's a hole down by the creek and a couple more on the hill that show a lot of sign." Dad smiled. I could tell he was impressed by my wealth of knowledge and extensive research of the natural habitat.

"Pick out some traps and I'll help you set the first one."

I pulled six, double-spring, number two steel traps from the pegs next to the doorway and threw them over my shoulder. Off down the holler we headed to a well-worn hole beneath a rock ledge just above the creek bed.

"Dig out a little spot as close to the hole as possible for the trap to sit," instructed Dad. Heck, I already knew that, but figured I'd humor him since he'd been good enough to loan me the hardware to catch my fortune.

"Always make sure the chain is anchored to a bush or something heavy they can't drag off." He pulled a pair of pliers from the leg pocket of his overalls and secured the chain to a large root with a double strand of heavy wire. "I don't want 'em running off with my traps."

I leaned forward and nodded like I was hanging on every word. Who did he think he was talking to—a rookie? After setting the trigger, we gently placed the trap into the cavity I'd prepared, covered it with a light layer of leaves, and backed off to admire our handiwork.

"Looks pretty good," said Dad. "I'll go tend to the milking while you set the rest of your traps."

Lying in bed that night, I visualized running my traps. All six would be filled with top-grade wooly mammoths. It would take two, maybe three trips to carry in my catch, and I would likely need a wheelbarrow to cart my new found income to the Five & Dime where I would spend it all on candy and defective plastic objects fresh off the ship from Taiwan.

Saturday morning I was up and dressed before Mom could even bang on my door. After breakfast, I zipped through my chores in record time and strapped on Dad's .22 revolver like Wyatt Earp on his way to the Arcade Corral to shoot it out with that Clanton kid who hijacked the pinball machine.

"Oh, by the way," said Dad. "Minnie Pearl bayed a skunk last night on top of the hill above your trap line. It's lying next to the old barn if you want it. Probably be worth a dollar or two."

I thanked him and went on my way. Skunk odor wasn't that offensive to me personally, but I expected to have critters of higher value waiting in my traps. Besides, who wanted to wear a skunk? People of means wore raccoon coats, mink stoles, and other fancy furs. You never heard of anyone clamoring for a skunk sport coat or a black and white striped collar to accent their silk smoking jacket. The only potential market I could think of was politicians. A skunk-skin cap would be a perfect fit for their profession and would make it easier to tell the two parties apart. Democrats would wear theirs with the tail hanging down the back, donkey-fashion, and Republicans could spin it around and go elephant style.

My dog, Jo Jo, a full size, Lassie-look-alike, had accompanied me on the trap setting expedition. He was bouncing like a toddler on a sugar high as we headed out to run the line. I'm sure he'd spent all night dreaming of our success and couldn't wait to see how much of my new found wealth would be spent on him.

We ran all the way to the creek. When the set under the rock ledge came into view I couldn't believe my eyes. There was no raccoon, mink, or other fine-furred creature in our trap. How could this be? Didn't these critters understand their role in the grand scheme of things?

The first two sets at the crest of the hill showed no sign of activity, either. We were oh-for-three, and I was becoming frustrated. My ever-faithful companion, Jo Jo, began straying further from my side as if he were embarrassed to be seen with such a sorry excuse for a trapper.

But like good soldiers we marched on together to the next set. This natural den ran beneath a boulder the size of a Rambler station wagon. Jo Jo's ears sprang to attention and he darted toward the hole. I felt a rush of excitement. He barked out, "Woof, woof. Woof, woof!" which translated means, "We've got one. We've got one!"

Approaching the trap from the downhill side, I peered into the hole. The only part of the critter I could see was its rear end. Unfortunately, it was just like our TV—black and white. This meant one thing. I had to shoot it before it shot us. Drawing my trusty revolver from its holster, I squinted one eye and took careful aim down the barrel.

"Spat," rang the pistol. The speeding bullet had barely escaped the muzzle when Jo Jo leapt between me and the skunk, determined to wrestle the critter from the hole like yankin' a rotten molar from the clutches of the Redneck Tooth Fairy.

His timing couldn't have been worse, or his mouth open any wider. A stream of yellow liquid hit the back of Jo Jo's throat with such force it knocked him off his feet. He rolled on his back, mouth frozen in gag-reflex mode, eyes bulging from their sockets. Scrambling to his feet, he coughed, spat, slobbered, and hacked like a four-pack-a-day smoker. His sides pumped like a blacksmith's bellows, straining to fill his lungs with something other than the stench that infested his mouth.

After an eternity of five or six minutes (probably five or six lifetimes to him), Jo Jo regained his composure and turned on the skunk with vengeance. This time he took a different angle, steering clear of the rear quarters. Once satisfied the skunk's spraying days were over, Jo Jo dropped it at my feet and trotted down the trail toward the next trap.

The next two sets had not been thrown. I remembered the skunk Dad told me about by the barn. I hadn't really planned on fooling with it, but now that I had the scent on me, one more wasn't going to make it any worse.

Dad was piddling outside the shop and turned when he saw me, arms extended, carrying a skunk in each hand.

"I hate to tell you this, Son," he said, "but your cologne arrived before you did." Dad chuckled and I returned a half-grin. His attempt at humor didn't strike me as funny under the circumstances.

"There's a trick to skinning skunks," said Dad. "The first thing you want to do is cut out the scent gland. He had me hold one of the skunks upside down, hind legs wide apart. "Here, I'll show you how on this one." Dad inserted his pocket knife below the tail and with a flick of his wrist cut a perfect circle in one smooth motion. Pinching a sliver of skin between his finger and thumb, he gently lifted a pouch-like bag, slightly smaller than a golf ball, from the skunk and tossed it on the ground.

"There you go. Now, you can cut it out on the next one." Satisfied that he had imparted adequate instruction and fatherly advice, Dad headed to the house to share the news of my glorious catch with Mom.

I finished removing the pelt from skunk number one and picked up number two. Grabbing an old shoestring, I anchored one hind leg to a peg on the doorpost and held the other leg in my left hand. With the precision of a Hollywood plastic surgeon, my blade plunged into the narrow cavity between the pelvic bones. The video inside my head replayed the smooth, swift motion of Dad's wrist as his knife encircled the gland. In that moment of supreme confidence, I flicked my wrist.

But something went dreadfully wrong. A substance the consistency of syrup and the color of golden sunflowers slithered down the blade of my knife. I had time for one final breath before all oxygen was depleted from northern hemisphere. Caustic fumes rose from the epicenter of the catastrophe and sent neighbors as far as two farms away scurrying for the safety of a fallout shelter.

There I stood, the lone survivor at ground zero, eyes burning, knife in hand, puffed up like a blowfish holding my breath. Wave after wave of after-shock hammered the breeze, but I remained at my post, determined to finish the job or die a martyr—whichever came first.

By the time skunk number two was finished, I'd grown so accustomed to the odor that the smell was no longer offensive. In fact, nothing seemed to affect my olfactory system. There were no good smells, bad smells, or ordinary smells. There was only one smell, and it ruled the entire planet.

Mom met me at the backdoor. A clean shirt, pants, and underwear dangled from an outstretched arm extending through a narrow crack between the door and jamb. Tennis shoes, socks, a washcloth, and soap sat waiting on the steps.

"You're not coming in here smelling like that," she said. "Now, go up to the old house and clean yourself up. And BE SURE and leave your old clothes up there. They need to air out for a week or two."

The icy water from the well raised a harvest of goose bumps on my tender flesh. Late November was no time for an impromptu bath without the comfort of heat or warm water. I wondered if other trapping legends had to put up with this kind of treatment from their mothers. Slipping into my sweet-smelling clean clothes, I tied my tennis shoes and raced off to the house to see what was for dinner.

Looking back on my skunk experience, I realize that people can argue from here to kingdom come about the moral issues associated with hunting and trapping. There are two sides to every story and a person would do well to listen closely to both before falling too much in love with either. As for me, there's one thing I can say with absolute certainty, there's more than one way to skin a skunk.

Manufactured Tales

Somewhere in that mess of twisted caverns between my ears there's a little factory that cranks out stories. Everyone who works in this plant suffers from some form of mental disorder. The assembly line runs in a serpentine pattern before passing through a broken-down oven which provides that "half-baked" effect which has become the trademark of their finished products.

The Peterinarian

"I'm Frank Forester. Welcome to *Voyages into the Unknown*. Tonight we continue our series on unusual occupations. Dr. Winfred Bonham, author and acclaimed physician in the field of Peterinary Medicine, is our guest.

Dr. Bonham, welcome to the show. You are one of only four practicing Peterinarians in the world. Tell us a little bit about your profession and how you became interested in this field."

"Thank you, Frank. Peterinary Medicine is a relatively new, but rapidly growing scientific community. The world is a much different place today than it was fifty or sixty years ago. Lifestyles have changed. Population growth and the urbanization of society have made it increasingly difficult for many people to own and care for conventional pets, such as dogs and cats.

In the late 1960s and early 70s scientists discovered that a variety of stone species that could be domesticated for companionship. The two most common, and well known, were Pet Rocks and Mood Rings. Some of the obvious advantages of these pets were that they adapted well to almost any environment, low maintenance requirements, and that owners did not have to clean up feces.

Over the past two decades, advances in computer science have led to the creation and development of ePets. As electronic devices became portable and affordable, more people expressed interest in virtual companions."

"Can these types of pets become ill and require medical attention, Dr. Bonham?"

"Absolutely. A common misconception is that these pets do not have physical and emotional needs."

"I can't help but notice that Peterinarian sounds a lot like Veterinarian. Would you explain the difference to our audience?"

"I'd be happy to, Frank. Not long after people began keeping domesticated stones as pets, a variety of problems started to occur. One of the earliest reported cases was a woman in New Jersey who noticed the complexion of her Pet Rock, Wilbur, had turned from his normal sandy-brown color to olive green. She also complained of an odor, similar to a rotten egg, emanating from the stone. The medical community, veterinarians in particular, ignored her cry for help – refusing to treat any pet that did not eat, drink, or have a pulse."

"That's horrible, Dr. Bonham. Was she able to find help for Wilbur?"

"Fortunately, Dr. Johann Douche' (pronounced Dou-shay), a German physician, who also held a degree in psychology, heard about the case and offered his assistance.

She flew Wilbur to Frankfurt for an examination. After extensive testing and evaluation Dr. Douche' diagnosed him with a severe case of gallitosis.

Wilbur had spent an excessive amount of time on the bathroom counter. Exposure to harsh cleaning chemicals, toothpaste, perfumes, hairspray, and toxic odors from a nearby water closet, contributed to the manifestation of this disease.

Dr. Douche' recommended bathing him for thirty minutes daily in a solution of one part vinegar and three parts distilled water for five days. He also prescribed a regime of four to six hours of direct sunlight per week.

The patient displayed noticeable improvement after only two treatments. The foul odor dissipated and his color returned to normal within a few short days."

"That's amazing, Dr. Bonham. Can we assume that Dr. Douche' was the first pioneer to brave this new frontier?"

"Yes, without a doubt. He is considered the Father of Peterinary Medicine, and was my personal mentor. I studied under him for two years and we remained close until his passing in 2004."

"Earlier, you mentioned Mood Rings. My girlfriend in college wore one throughout her freshman and sophomore years. Would you elaborate on some of the problems people have experienced with these stones?"

"Mood Rings were popular for a brief period of time, particularly with young women, such as your girlfriend. Problems arose when owners treated them as an accessory, or piece of jewelry. They failed to recognize the stones as pets, and that they required a higher level of care and attention.

Repeated abuse and neglect caused many Mood stones to become resentful of their owners. Instead of accurately reflecting the mood of the wearer, the stones began to impose their will upon the attitude of their owner. A young woman might be in a happy, cheerful mood, slip on her ring and turn into a She-Devil.

There are six documented cases of young men who were killed by their girlfriends, or wives, who were wearing a Mood Ring at the time of the murder."

"That explains a lot about the sudden change in my girl-friend's personality. Is there any way to keep a Mood Ring from turning on its owner?"

"The treatment is actually quite simple. Dr. Douche' developed a special rubber pouch for removing evil thoughts from the stones. Pour three to four ounces of hydrogen peroxide into the pouch and place the ring inside. Flush the stone by gently squeezing the sides of the pouch, forcing the solution back and forth around the ring. Rinse in warm water and it's ready to wear.

"Owners should clean their rings at least three times a week to keep the stones happy and healthy. The rubber pouches, known as Douche' bags, can be purchased online or at any store that sells Peterinary supplies."

"Dr. Bonham, there has been an explosion of interest in ePets lately. A lot of articles have been written promoting them, and ePet stores are popping up all over the internet. Would you give our audience some advice on the selection and care of virtual pets?"

"ePets make wonderful companions, Frank. My wife has an ePoodle, Blanche, and I have an eBulldog named Winston. They love to travel. We take them everywhere we go.

"If you have a PC or laptop, you may want an eRabbit, an eButterfly, or something of that nature. Writers tend to be fond of eInchworms, as they can be trained to measure copy, perform word count, and other helpful tasks.

"Owners of touch-screen devices, such as iPhones, enjoy eDogs and eCats. Winston loves to have me rub his belly and scratch behind his ears.

"ePets, like other Apps, are susceptible to viruses. You must be extremely careful if you take your pet to an ePark. Many owners do not recognize the early symptoms of these diseases and may unwittingly expose other animals in virtual playgrounds. When shopping for virus protection make sure that it provides coverage specifically related to ePet illnesses."

"Thank you, Dr. Bonham. That brings us to the call-in portion of our show. We have Sally, from Traverse City, Michigan on the line. Go ahead, Sally."

"Thank you for taking my call.

"Dr. Bonham, I have a cyber-snake, Stanley, who has not been himself lately. He used to slither out of his icon, rise erect in the middle of my screen, and softly hiss at me – winking one eye.

"I read a lot of romance novels on my Kindle. Stanley used to pop-up and surprise me during the most heated, passionate passages of the story. But recently, he seems to have lost all interest in love scenes and lies limp at the bottom of the screen with a sad look on his face."

"What would you estimate Stanley's age to be, Sally?"

"Well, I've had him about five years. When I adopted him from the ePet Rescue Shelter they told me he was four years old."

"Nine is past middle-age for a male cyber-snake. Without examining him personally, I can only speculate on this medical condition. The behavior you describe is consistent with the symptoms of eReptile Dysfunction. His loss of interest and inability to perform to your expectations are affecting his sense of worth. Depression is often a result of low self-esteem.

"The good news, Sally, is that there are medications available that have proven effective in treating this condition. The majority of patients report a high level of satisfaction, both for themselves and their companions. Contact my office and make an appointment for your pet."

"Thank you, Dr. Bonham. I can't wait to tell Stanley!"

"Well, folks, we're all out of time. I'd like to thank our guest, Dr. Winfred Bonham, for joining us this evening. Be sure and tune in next week when psychic Antoinette Dubois will reveal the mysteries of near-death experiences on *Voyages into the Unknown*. I'm Frank Forester. Goodnight."

The Perils of Heavy Thinking

"Thinking is the hardest work there is; which is probably the reason why so few engage in it." – Henry Ford

Last year, the necessity arose for me to visit a physician. I was not a new patient, yet they forced me to fill out the same mountain of paperwork as if I had never seen a doctor before. This seems hypocritical and unnecessary, since they are always bragging about how they are up to snuff on the latest and greatest technical and scientific equipment available to the medical community. All this technology at their fingertips and they can't even keep up with my name, address, and who to notify in case I die in their office while being diagnosed with an ingrown hangnail. But, these folks have taken a Hypocritical Oath, so why should I expect them to practice what they preach?

On page thirty-two, section D, line fourteen, they ask how many alcoholic drinks you consume daily. I find this line of questioning a little discriminatory. They don't ask how many donuts or slices of fried bacon you had for breakfast, both of which (according to doctors) are supposed to be detrimental to your health. Neither do they ask about your good habits, such as how many servings of fruit, vegetables, and hearty grains you average per day. Evidently, the logic here is if you can live on wild berries, hickory nuts, and poke salad, you won't be showing up in their office to begin with.

An even more serious omission on the questionnaire was the failure to capture data relating to one's thought patterns. Millions of people suffer serious injury, even death, every year due to Heavy Thinking. This debilitating disease has been known to cause migraine headaches, stimulate the growth of gray hair (or baldness), and create an artificial illusion of intelligence. Repeated Heavy Thinking (i.e. Chronic Thinking) can be a "gateway" to more dangerous activities such as; analytical problem solving, philosophy, and a compulsive addiction to watch reruns of Jeopardy.

Thinking and driving don't mix either. My friend, David, got arrested the other day for failure to proceed at a green light. According to the officer's report, the light had cycled three times while David sat motionless, backing up traffic for eight blocks. After reviewing his license and registration, the officer asked, "Sir, have you been Thinking?"

"No," replied David, rather indignantly.

"Then you won't mind taking a brain-wave field sobriety test," said the officer. He plucked a gadget about the size of an iPhone from his shirt pocket, clamped the positive lead to David's left ear and the negative to his right. David stared at the visor and tried to clear his mind.

"Uh-huh," said the officer, after clicking the 'save' icon. "Step out of the car, please."

The next thing David knew he was being fingerprinted and booked for DWT (Driving While Thinking).

"Mr. Franklin," said the judge. "Why didn't you drive forward when the light turned green?"

"Well, Your Honor, I thought . . . ."

"Ah ha!" screamed the prosecuting attorney. "He admits it. He THOUGHT!"

"Bang!" slammed the judge's gavel. "Mr. Franklin, this court finds you guilty as charged."

After paying a hefty fine and attending a six-week course on thought-free driving, David finally got his license back.

Unfortunately, his auto insurance premium doubled, and his employer, Evergreen Lawns, banned him from riding mowers.

"The last thing we need," bellowed Sam Lewis, owner of Evergreen, "is to have some idiot thinking while operating one of our zero-turn mowers. Franklin, you are relegated to weed-eaters and push mowers till you get this *thinking* problem of yours under control."

It pains me to say this, but one group at high risk for Heavy Thinking addiction is writers. These individuals spend a lot of time alone in front of blank computer screens, actually *encouraging* the thought process. If they would spend more time with family and friends enjoying mindless activities, such as watching television or babbling incoherently about nothing in particular, the world would be a safer place.

But no! They like to push the envelope. Not only are *they* Heavy Thinkers, they want to drag readers down to their level by making them think too. To make matters worse, they form little groups and hold regular meetings. Sometimes they even invite well-known Heavy Thinkers from big cities to come and pro-pound thought-provoking advice under the guise of a "conference."

Last spring I attended one of these "conferences" and let me tell you, there was a whole lot of Heavy Thinking going on. By the time the keynote speaker finished his address the entire audience was intoxicated on knowledge. They spent the next day and a half scheming new ideas and plotting future confer-ences. I was appalled at such a blatant display of public Thinking. What a shame to desecrate such a fine hotel.

As part of my research on Heavy Thinking, I began attending some of these small group meetings. Not to brag, but I can say with complete confidence that I have far fewer thoughts than any of the other members. During the critique session, a Heavy Thinker will offer a fledgling writer a double-shot of powerful suggestions to improve his story. The conversation continues around the room until everyone has contributed meaningful advice. By now, the author of said paper is showing signs of dizziness and becoming quite inebriated. I usually sit there with that deer in the headlights look, occasionally offering half a thought – just to be social.

One place you won't find any Heavy Thinking is in a bar. If a patron starts showing signs of forming a thought, an eight-foot bouncer with Popeye arms and the disposition of an angry badger will grab the offender by the scruff of the neck and toss him out the door. Once ejected from the establishment, he'd better hope a cop doesn't come along. He might suffer the same fate as poor David.

A lot of people have asked me for guidance in determining if a loved one has a serious Thinking problem. Here are some of the warning signs.

☺ Denial — "Sure, I may have a thought or two from time to time, but hey, I know my limit. I can quit any time I want."

☺ Response to Yes/No questions — A non-Thinker will immediately answer Yes or No. Heavy Thinkers will spend several minutes analyzing the question, followed by an extended period in which they formulate a three-paragraph response. By the time they come back with an answer, you've forgotten what the question was.

☺ Problems at work — Heavy Thinkers can't just come in, do their jobs and go home. That would be too easy. They start questioning processes, making suggestions, and complicating everyone's lives. Pretty soon, they've been promoted to supervisor – then the real trouble starts.

☺ Constantly making excuses to think — "It relaxes me, it's how I unwind," or, "just a thought or two after dinner never hurt anyone."

☺ Angry when confronted — "Damn right I think. That's why God gave me a brain."

☺ Thinking at unusual hours — I hate to keep picking on writers, but I've heard several of these poor souls confess to Thinking before they even get out of bed. No wonder Hemingway committed suicide.

If you, or someone you love, has a serious Thinking problem, please get help now. Call 1-888-NO THINK. Trained counselors are standing by twenty-four hours a day.

Don't Think yourself to an early grave.

Call now.

Take the first step toward becoming thought free. In just a few short weeks you could be enjoying the freedom and bliss of total, unadulterated ignorance.

Why wait?

Call today.

Do it for someone you love. You'll be glad you did.

Much Nothing About Ado

Have you ever been accused of rambling? Are you the kind of person who likes to talk just to hear his head rattle? Me neither.

People like us don't mince words. We cut to the chase – get right to the point. If you ask us what time it is, we're not going to spend half a day telling you how to build a watch. I could go on and on about how clear and concise we communicate, but there's no need to preach to the choir.

My friend, Leonard on the other hand, is a different story. The seasons changed from spring to fall and into the next summer while he told me about his recent trip to Walmart for a bottle of aspirin. I had to interrupt him before he got to the end to see if he actually got the aspirin. My head was pounding like the bass drum at a Metallica concert, and I could tell it would take at least two more weeks to get to the "good part," as he likes to call it.

Leonard's stories always start in the middle. In this instance he droned on for a couple of hours about the cute little pharmacy assistant and their lengthy debate over the virtues of name brand versus store brand, followed by the pros and cons of tablets, capsules, and powders. I'm sure the poor girl must have missed two breaks and her lunch hour before she figured out how to get away from him.

Just when I thought he was about to reach a decision on which aspirin to buy, he jumped to the beginning of the story.

No, I don't mean the part where he arrived at Walmart and started looking for a parking spot – no, no – much earlier than that.

He began at sunrise, walked me through breakfast, gave a play-by-play description of the argument he had with his wife about the hole in his favorite plaid dress shirt, and finished act one by telling me that the nylon zipper on his khaki pants kept popping open every time he bent over or sat down.

The first time I heard one of Leonard's stories I tried to be patient and polite. After a couple of hours, I glanced repeatedly at my wrist watch, hoping he'd get the hint. He noticed all right.

"Nice watch," he said. "That reminds me of the time..." and off he went into another thrilling tale of watching water boil or waiting for paint to peel.

I kept looking for an opening where I could inject an excuse to leave gracefully, but Leonard has the amazing ability to inhale while talking.

Maybe I should just kill him. It would be self-defense. No jury would convict me. I'd be doing society a favor.

Even if it was justifiable homicide, I couldn't bring myself to kill Leonard – at least not at that moment. He deserves something more devious and horrible than simple murder. It has to be slow and torturous, like what he puts me through.

"You'll never guess what happened then," said Leonard, snapping me out of my trance.

"No, I don't –"

"When I got to the check-out counter I noticed the dad-gum tamper-evident seal was broken." Leonard was not going to let me complete a thought, let alone a sentence. He just wanted to reaffirm my presence before he went on with the aspirin adventure.

Leonard's not a bad person. He'd give you the shirt off his back. If you needed help in the middle of the night, he'd get out of bed, put on a gasoline suit, and walk through the flames of

Hell to come to your rescue. It's just that he's so damned annoying. No one can stand to be around him for any length of time.

Several times he's asked me if my wife knew any nice single girls she could fix him up with. I didn't have the heart to tell him that we don't know any deaf/mute females, so I said, "I don't think so. All her friends are married."

Leonard is so kind and thoughtful that if he dated a deaf/mute girl he'd probably learn sign language and drive her crazy within six months. I can see him now, waving his arms around and making exaggerated facial expressions while explaining the wonders of self-adhesive postage stamps.

We're now into the eighth month of the aspirin story (I've been timing it with a calendar). Leonard tells me we're almost to the "good part." The anticipation is killing me. I dust the cobwebs from my neck and ears in preparation for this thrilling event.

"Come to find out," said Leonard. "I went to school with the daughter of the lady at the check-out counter. We even had a couple of dates. You just never know who you are going to run into at Walmart."

That's the good part? Can I choke him now?

I began to wonder what percentage of my life had been wasted listening to long-winded stories that had no meaning or point.

Two hours later the epic saga came to a startling conclusion. Leonard arrived home with aspirin in hand, only to discover that he no longer had a headache.

Well . . . imagine that.

"Where have you been? I was starting to get worried," my wife said, when I finally arrived home. "You look worn out. Did you have a rough day at work?"

"No. I ran into Leonard when I stopped at the Quickie Mart for gas."

"Oh, you poor dear. Let me get you some extra-strength Excedrin and a cold beer."

Now, that's what I call a good woman. She said everything I wanted to hear in two short, sweet sentences. I think I'll keep her.

Life with Mona

"Mona, I'm home." Ron turned and locked the front door behind him. Mona was leaning back in the recliner, bare feet pointing toward the ceiling, staring blindly at the TV.

"Watching Jerry Springer again?" He chuckled. It was a rhetorical question. Mona spent every day in front of the TV. Game shows, talk shows, soap operas, it didn't matter. She was even mesmerized by the commercials for hemorrhoid creams and toilet paper.

Mona didn't cook or clean either. Ron knew that before she moved in. He didn't mind. Besides, he was kind of picky about those sorts of things. Co-workers had even accused him of having an obsessive compulsive disorder. Maybe he was a little eccentric – but a disorder? Never!

Ron had always felt like a square peg. Talking to women, even making eye contact, was especially difficult. His attempts to ask girls out always ended in failure – usually without the question ever being asked.

He used to spend days, sometimes weeks, plotting how and where to approach women. Smiling at the mirror, he would rehearse sexy come-on lines and seductive body language like the studs on TV.

But when show-time arrived, Ron's spine became a bowl of quivering Jello. The inside of his mouth turned to cotton, sweat poured from every orifice, and his stomach churned like an erupting volcano – usually resulting in a spew.

With Mona everything was different. Ron could be himself. He didn't have to worry about what to say, or do. She never criticized him or scrutinized behaviors that others considered odd or unusual.

If he came home late, it was no big deal. She would look at him with those big brown eyes, ruby lips forming a perfect circle, as if to say, "Oh, Ron, I'm so glad to see you."

Her cheerful demeanor never changed. They didn't argue or fight. In fact, they rarely spoke at all. Life with Mona was a happy escape from the relentless pressures of a harsh and cruel world.

Ron had introduced her to his immediate family and a couple of his closest friends. None of them seemed to really hit it off. His Mother had even made a nasty remark about them living together.

Ron didn't care. What gave them the right to be so judgmental? Just thinking about it pissed him off.

"They can kiss my ass," he told Mona.

Tonight was their anniversary, one full year of joyful bliss. The bouquet of roses he picked up on the way home created a beautiful centerpiece for the small square table in the corner of the kitchen. Ron prepared an elegant candlelight dinner and poured them both a glass of chardonnay.

After the meal they moved to the couch. Ron put on some soft, romantic, music to set the mood, settled in beside her, and pulled her body close.

"Baby, I'll never forget the first time I saw you – your jet black hair hanging like silk on your shoulders. The way your eyes followed me as I walked around the room. Your cheeks blushing under the red neon of the 'Open' sign."

Ron ran his fingers through her hair, down her slender neck, and began caressing her bare shoulders.

"I had to make you mine," he whispered. "Get you away from that place. I couldn't stand the way those other men were looking at you. They wanted to treat you like a toy – abuse you. I couldn't let that happen. No one could love you like I do."

He leaned over and began kissing the nape of her neck, working his way down one side to her bosom, over to the other, and back up.

"Honey, are you feeling a little low tonight? Let me see if I can help."

Ron flicked the stopper of the valve-stem with his tongue, grasped it between his teeth and pulled it open. Wrapping his lips around the stem he blew two deep breaths into her body. He could feel her bosom swell and become firm against his.

"That's my girl," he purred.

"Happy Anniversary, Sweetheart."

Stolen Goods

Burglary is a common occurrence at our house. How he gets in, steal what he wants, and gets out without leaving a single clue indicates true professionalism. The doors haven't been jimmied, the windows remain closed and locked, and yet numerous items continue to disappear. In fact, this thief is so clever and subtle, it's darned near impossible to prove the missing articles ever existed.

Notifying the authorities is an exercise in futility and a waste of cell phone minutes. We've had the cops out a couple times. The county dispatches a glum-looking deputy who documents our complaint, scratches a few undecipherable notes on a yellow pad, and promises to patrol the area on a semi-bi-monthly basis – if and when – staffing and funds become available.

The only known witness to these crimes is Buster, our dog. I have interrogated him on numerous occasions and suspect he may be in collusion with the criminal. How he can look me square in the eye and refer to himself as a "guard dog" confirms his total lack of respect for the job title.

The tom-thievery in our neighborhood began several years ago, about the time my father started displaying early signs of dementia. Dad, who lived in the next house up the road, noticed a pair of rubber boots was missing. Three minutes and one phone call later, my wife, Connie, and I were enlisted to join the search-and-rescue squad. We spent hours combing hazardous terrain, fighting brutal cobwebs and a relentless army of dust bunnies. The boots could not be found.

My sweet and naïve mother, who always thought the best of everyone, insisted the boots were merely misplaced and would eventually turn up. Dad was livid.

"Hell, no! They were stolen."

The thief had no need for guns, tools, electronics, or precious gems that might weigh him down. No! He had been coveting a used pair of size nine rubber boots for some time, lying in wait for the right moment to sweep down and snatch them for his own. Dad could just picture some guy stomping down the driveway, pant legs tucked in the boots, grinning like he'd won the lottery.

Two months later, Mom decided to shampoo the carpet and asked me to help move the couch. It was then we discovered that we were dealing with the most vile and hideous type of criminal. One who would not only invade your home to steal rubber boots, but who would also break in just to bring them back.

Despite keeping a vigilant eye on personal belongings, items continued to disappear. Some would eventually return with little or no damage while others – primarily food-stuff, such as pies, cakes, and candy – never made it back. It was impossible to predict when the thief would strike, but we determined the best way to protect a pie was to cut it into sections and wrap our stomachs around the individual slices.

After Mom and Dad passed away, Connie and I bought their house, remodeled it, and rented it to a young couple. The thief who had long coveted Phillips screwdrivers, tubs of margarine, and partial rolls of crochet thread, no longer took an interest in items at this address. Instead, he chose to move his operation to the next house down the road – ours.

Those who study such things will tell you that intelligent criminals target specific demographics. Much like predators in the animal kingdom, they seek easy marks who are unable to protect themselves. This list includes the very young, those with physical or mental deficiencies, and of course (gulp) the elderly.

There seems to be an ongoing debate regarding the age at which one officially becomes classified as "elderly." If you ask a ten year old, the number is thirty. If you ask a sixty year old, it's eighty-four. If you ask our thief (notice how we've assumed personal ownership), the transformation occurs when your first AARP membership application comes in the mail.

Evidently, he had been staking out our mailbox for some time, anxiously awaiting the moment our elderliness would arrive. By the time Connie made the short walk from the mailbox to the front door, things were already starting to disappear. Before the ink was dry on the application, we were down one flashlight, a fly swatter, two caramel apples, and my favorite *Calvin & Hobbes* cartoon book. It was a good thing AARP included a postage paid return envelope because the stamps were gone too.

I'd like to say he never takes anything of real value, but the sparkle of diamonds and glitter of gold lose their luster when you're stranded on a toilet and the half-roll of paper that was resting within arm's reach two minutes ago gets stolen the second you glance out the window. Such thievery causes one to stop and reevaluate priorities.

Over the years, as my hair has grown a more flattering shade of silver, I've become so used to our thief's antics that I expect things to be missing when I look for them. There is one exception – tools. On several occasions, when Connie has a project scheduled for me, I have left tools in plain sight (his favorite place) to make them easy to pilfer, but he refuses to steal them. Either he, Connie, or Buster are in cahoots (bribed with pie and milk bones, I suspect), or the thief is even *more* opposed to work than I am.

The Dave Barry Experience

"We were *that close*," said JB. His forefinger and thumb spread apart the width of a blonde belly-hair. "I can't believe that camera girl ran off after I gave her money." His face flushed with anger and his eyes turned to photographer-seeking missiles beneath a furrowed brow. Determined to locate her, he circled the room in long accentuated strides like Groucho Marx, minus the cigar. She could not be found.

I looked at Dave Barry and smiled. *Oh well, maybe next time.*

Another visitor stepped up to shake hands and rub elbows with the Funniest Man in America (according to the New York Times). Dave appeared cordial, but I could tell underneath that mask of professionalism, he was deeply hurt and disappointed.

Earlier in the evening, during our introductions, JB Hogan, my cousin and fellow writer, informed Mr. Barry that many people considered me to be the Dave Barry of Northwest Arkansas. To which Mr. Barry replied, "That's interesting. Everyone considers me the Russell Gayer of South Florida."

Dave noticed I had one of his books, *I'll Mature When I'm Dead*, tucked under my arm. "Can I sign that for you?" he begged.

"Sure, that would be nice."

"Is it Russell with two S's and two L's?"

"Yes, and you'd be surprised how many people can't spell it correctly."

"Well, I want to make sure I get it right," he said, throwing open the book to the title page and scrawling his little note.

I was about to share some tips on writing humor with Dave when a porky, ex-politician shoved his way to the front of the line and interrupted our conversation. The only time those guys show any consideration is before you go in the voting booth. After election day, you're just another grape to be trampled in the vineyard of life.

Dave handled the situation with grace and dignity. He smiled, nodded his head, and shook the old boy's hand like he really gave a crap what the guy was saying. I was impressed at how well he concealed his disappointment about missing out on the humor tips.

"What'd he write?" asked JB. I opened the book and showed him.

To Russell, my idol. – Dave Barry.

"Hey . . . that's cool," said JB. I could tell he was envious. It's a good thing I'm such a humble person. A lot of people would let a compliment like Dave wrote go to their heads.

After the missed photo op, we all went downstairs to hear Dave speak. We'd been seated ten or fifteen minutes when he finally walked into the room. Evidently, he needed some time to regain his composure after missing out on having his picture made with two of the finest authors in Northwest Arkansas. I felt bad for him, but the guy's a real trooper. He kept the audience in stitches for an entire hour without showing how distraught he was over the photo. JB found out later that Dave went to Dickson Street after the show and drowned his sorrow in cold beer.

I wish things could've turned out differently. There's a big, bare spot on Dave's web site that would've been the perfect place for a picture of the three of us and it would have provided a shot in the arm for his career.

Hell, I might even have posted it on *my* blog.

Mallard P.I.

One Saturday, while reading my favorite magazine, *The Nasty Inquirer,* the phone rang. It was a woman. She wanted me to come right over. Said she needed my help, but couldn't discuss it over the phone.

Probably just another dizzy dame who wanted to curl my tail feathers, but what the heck, I decided to play along. Besides, I needed the money.

When the cabbie dropped me off I gave him a tip. "Invest in plastics." That's my favorite line from *The Graduate* and I use it every chance I get. He drove away cussing. Some people just don't appreciate a good tip.

She was alone. One look told me that she had all the right equipment and knew how to use it.

"Hello, Madame. Mallard's the name. You wanted to see me?"

"Oh, Mallard," she said, in a cute little quack. "I'm so glad you came!"

Her name was Mary. Tears streamed down her pretty speckled cheeks as she sobbed her sad story. By the time she was done, we were swimming in a pool of salt water. It seems someone had been sabotaging her operation. A spineless snake was siphoning off every penny of profit, creating large gaps in her cash flow, and causing unsightly bags under her gorgeous brown eyes.

"Mary," I said. "Give me a week on the payroll and we'll catch this slime ball." I quoted her my usual rate. After all, a duck has to make a buck.

"Oh, Mallard," she cooed, "If you can save my business, I'll gladly give you anything you want." Those words hovered in the air like a Goodyear Blimp above the Super Bowl. Obviously, she was not familiar with my reputation (or . . . maybe she was).

I showed up for work Monday morning dressed in dirty coveralls. Mary told the employees that I was the new maintenance man. With bent-frame mirror-shades and dried mud caked on my webbed feet, I was sure no one would suspect my true occupation.

My plan was to get cozy with some of the employees, especially the ladies. Women love to talk. Flirt with them a little and they'll tell you anything you want to know, and a whole lot more you don't give a damn about.

One cute little hen invited me to lunch. Her name was Sharon. We sat down in a private booth at a little dive known as the Wetland Grill. While I munched on wild rice and soybeans, her pretty beak flapped in the breeze. She gave me the scoop on every employee. Their family histories, love lives, financial problems, more dirty laundry than Folsom Prison on wash day.

That night I met with Mary. "I've got a hunch about this case," I said. "But I'm going to need a small part of my fee before we can proceed." She jumped on me like a duck on a June bug. Within a couple of hours, I had received the first installment.

The rest of the week was spent collecting evidence. By Friday, I had enough hard facts to pin this bird. I clued Mary in, and together we confronted her accountant, a wimpy little fellow named Teal. He started shaking like a leaf when I revealed my true identity. Caught dead to right, he whined a confession while his wire-rimmed glasses vibrated against his bill.

Then he pulled a gun.

"Hit the deck, Mary!" I screamed, as he fired wildly in our direction. Throwing my wing around her, I pulled her to the floor behind a heavy wooden desk. We could hear the flipity-flop of his feet as he waddled from the room, attempting to get to his car.

I cut across the parking lot and tackled the little jerk around the ankles. Teal's bill popped hard against the pavement. Grabbing the wire-rimmed glasses from his beak, I tied his wings behind his back.

Mary called the cops. They had a cage ready for this bird– jailbird that is.

Teal still gets to work with numbers. He stamps them on license plates.

As for Mary, she's happy now. Her business is healthy and making a profit – and her love life is great. She offered me the accounting job, but I turned it down.

"I'm no good at numbers, Mary," I told her. "I'm only good at handling figures." She smiled and wagged her cute little tail feathers.

It hurt to tell Mary goodbye, but it's best not to get too close to the clients. After all, guns don't kill detectives . . . love does.

Deadeye Dick
& the Stranger from Coyote Gulch

Horsehead was a sorry excuse for a town. Only a few people remained after the silver mine petered out. One particular member of the populace was a lowlife by the name of Deadeye Dick. He said his Pappy gave him the name Deadeye because he was such a good shot, but most people figured it was because his left eye was locked in a constant stare at his nose.

Deadeye was a peculiar-acting fellow whose sole occupation was gambling. Lord knows he wasn't very good at it. Usually at the end of a long night of playing cards and drinking Deadeye would stagger back to his one room shanty – located directly behind the public outhouse – totally penniless.

Nobody knew for sure where Dick got his stake money, but every night he seemed to come up with a few dollars to lose. Some folks thought he got it from poor little Charlene who worked at the cat house across from the saloon. She had a face like the south end of a northbound steer and wasn't exactly a genius. However, if a man had four or five stiff shots, her looks always seem to improve to the point where she could make a living.

She thought a lot of old Deadeye even though she knew he was as sorry as the day was long. He'd often tell her how he was gonna hit the big jackpot someday, when in fact the only green he ever had to show was when he opened his mouth to smile.

Tuesday, the twelfth of June, started out like any other uneventful day in Horsehead. The sun came up, the working people went about their business and the loafers loafed. About two o'clock a horse and rider came trotting in from the south side.

The stranger was a handsome devil with a black shiny handlebar moustache. He wore a long dark coat and a fancy silk vest. On his right leg was strapped a pearl-handled Colt and the shine on his boots would put out a cat's eye at fifty yards.

Old Lady Nelson, the town gossip, happened to be standing in front of Wilson's mercantile when he rode by. He tipped his hat and offered a complimentary, "Afternoon, Ma'am." Her eyes widened to the size of saucers and her jaw fell to her chest. She was rendered temporarily speechless by the sunlight reflecting off the gold tooth on the right side of his smile. You can bet her dress tail didn't touch the back of her legs until she had all the old hens in town cackling. Pretty soon Horsehead was buzzing like a horsefly.

The stranger tied up his horse in front of the boarding house and went inside to see about a room and a meal. He signed the register as Jack Huntington and asked Widow Jones, the proprietress, what time supper would be served. Then he went up to his room to get a little rest.

Meanwhile, Deadeye was just crawling out of bed. He poured a little water into the wash pan and splashed his face a couple of times before drying off with an old rotten towel that had been hanging on the bedpost for about a year. He pulled on his boots and stood up to look at his reflection in the broken piece of mirror that hung over the wash pan. Picking up what was left of an old nickel comb he raked it across his head, carefully pulling the few remaining strands of hair over the growing bald spot on top. Then he picked up his old hat and gently lowered it onto his freshly groomed noggin.

"Think I'll go see Charlene," he mumbled as he headed down the empty street of Horsehead.

Word of the handsome stranger had already reached the cat house. The ladies were chattering and giggling like a bunch of schoolgirls getting ready for their first date. They slipped into their finest lace bloomers and best Sunday dresses and added just a touch of some expensive French perfume that had been imported all the way from St. Louis.

"What's going on here," asked Deadeye. "Did the circus come to town?"

Charlene proceeded to inform him of the events of the day and the financial implications of such an opportunity. Obviously, Jack Huntington was a man of some wealth and perhaps could be persuaded to part with some of it for proper services rendered.

"Humph," grunted Deadeye. Nevertheless, he knew better than to offer his opinion of Charlene's chances. After all, he still needed a few dollars for tonight's game.

"Tell you what, Honey" he drawled, "I bet this feller is a gambler. Now, you know I'm due for a hot streak. If you'll just loan me a few dollars I bet I can clean his clock at the poker table tonight and if he's got any money left after that you girls can have a shot at him."

Throwing any pretense of common sense and good judgment to the wind, she reluctantly agreed and reached into her coin purse for a twenty dollar gold piece.

"Now Charlene" he whispered, "This feller Jack is probably a high roller. I may need a little more bait to get him to take the hook." She quickly handed him another gold coin and rushed upstairs before he could negotiate further.

Content with forty dollars in his pocket, he headed across the street to the saloon.

There was a big crowd at the Yellow Dog, especially for a weeknight. All the regulars –Bill Johnson, Todd Patrick, Clem Henson, and his boys – were there. None of them said much about the stranger, but they all had about the same agenda as Deadeye Dick.

Four or five of them got a table in the corner and started playing nickel and dime hands as a warm up for what they perceived as the main event. Deadeye actually won a dollar or two before bowing out to take an "alley break." He was off to a good start and he didn't want to waste a hot streak on these two-bit locals. He had bigger fish to fry.

About eight-thirty the swinging doors parted and the guest of honor arrived in grand fashion. He looked much as Mrs. Nelson had described, but with a thin cigar stuffed in his mouth opposite the gold tooth.

He carried himself like a man schooled in social graces and a high level of self-confidence. Stepping to the bar, he ordered a bottle of Kentucky whiskey and a glass, then turned to watch the activity at the corner table. After observing two or three hands, he strode over to the table.

"Good evening, gentlemen. Would you be so kind as to allow a lonely traveler an opportunity to join you in this game of chance?" he asked.

"Why certainly, friend" offered Todd Patrick. "Pull ya up a chair. We're playing seven card stud, nothin's wild. Deadeye, you want in?"

"Well, I reckon" replied he, trying to be nonchalant.

Todd dealt the first hand and things went well for Deadeye. He wound up with two pair, Queens and sevens, which were enough to win the pot.

Conversation and booze flowed freely over the next hour with Jack Huntington relating that he was a cattleman from a place in New Mexico called Coyote Gulch. Nobody believed a word of it. He had the look of a gambler, a gunfighter, or both.

Jack was two thirds of the way through his bottle of whiskey when he suggested that they raise the stakes. Bill and Todd lost one more round before they decided it was getting too rich for their blood and bowed out. That left only Jack, Deadeye and Clem Henson.

By now the ladies from the cat house were starting to get impatient. They hadn't seen a single customer all night. All the men were hanging out at the Yellow Dog and no one seemed interested in female companionship. The girls were also chomping at the bit to get at Jack Huntington, and if he wouldn't come to them, then by golly, they would go to him.

The men were heavily embroiled in a high stakes hand when the ladies sashayed through the side door. (They had been politely asked NOT to come through the front entrance as it might interfere will the home life of some of the regular patrons!) Shaking their skirts and laughing loudly they did their best to draw the attention of every red-blooded man in the room.

Deadeye had drawn a King, Queen, and ten of hearts on the first deal. He bet ten bucks, which Clem quickly matched, but Jack raised them both by ten. You could see Clem's left eye start to twitch as he threw in another ten. Deadeye made his contribution, everyone discarded, and Jack dealt the final cards. The first one Deadeye peeked at was the Ace of Hearts. Unfortunately, the next one was a seven of spades.

He stared blankly at the cards then glanced across the table at Jack. Jack appeared to have his eyes locked in on someone, or something, across the room. Deadeye turned to his left and saw Charlene cheerfully swirling from table to table, flirting with customers, and returning lustful eye contact with Jack. Deadeye's blood began to boil.

"Are we gonna play cards or stare at whores?" he howled.

"What's your hurry, friend?" replied Jack, with a big gold-toothed smile shooting back across the table. "The night is young and we've got plenty of time for both."

Clem folded right off the bat. It was down to Jack and Deadeye. Knowing that his stake was dwindling, and it was now or never, Deadeye decided to go for broke and bluff. He opened with a twenty.

"Hey, little lady," Jack called to Charlene. "Why don't you come over to our table? I bet you're lucky. Maybe you could share a little of that luck with a lonesome stranger. Come sit on my lap while I finish this hand."

She batted her eyes like a smooth southern belle and made her way across the room to Jack's chair. Sinking softly onto his right knee she backed into his torso with a gentle wiggle.

Deadeye's nostrils flared and his temples throbbed. He was experiencing feelings that he'd never known before. Anger, hatred, and jealousy. To him this game was no longer about money. It was about Charlene.

"I'll meet your twenty and raise you twenty more," announced Jack as he slid his right arm around Charlene's waist.

"Call," answered Deadeye with a burning stare. "Whatta ya got?"

"Just Jacks. Like me, ha ha hah," laughed Huntington as he fanned the cards out on the table. Deadeye swallowed hard. Three large Js jumped from the table and into the pit of his stomach.

Charlene giggled with glee and threw her arms around Jack's neck as he raked the pot from the table. That was more than Deadeye could take.

"Charlene! Get off his lap!" he snarled, in a hateful demanding tone. The room suddenly became as silent as a morgue.

Jack lowered his eyebrows and glared across the table. "I don't know who you think you are, friend, but if the lady's comfortable she's welcome to sit right here as long as she'd like. She doesn't have to take orders from a green-toothed loser like you."

Deadeye shoved the table into Jack's stomach with all his might. Charlene fell to the floor and quickly scrambled for safety behind the bar. Jack dodged a right hook from Deadeye and threw the table aside which knocked Deadeye to his knees. The two men struggled to their feet and exchanged blows while the bartender did his best to herd them in the general vicinity of the front door. A swift jab to the gut followed by a strong upper cut sent Deadeye flying backwards through the swinging doors and into the dusty street.

Jack followed him out, intent on finishing the job. He drew his revolver and fired. The bullet ripped through the left side of Deadeye's shirt, but barely grazed his ribs. He dove behind a nearby water trough just as shots two and three cut through water and wood.

Jack cautiously circled the end of the water trough like a cat toying with a rattlesnake. There was little moon that night and the only light in the street was from a smoldering torch hung from the facing of the saloon door. Deadeye crouched in the shadow of the trough and pounced on Jack as he rounded the corner. They wrestled fiercely in the darkness, struggling for control of the gun. Finally a shot rang out, then two. Both men lay motionless in the dust.

The saloon crowd had been anxiously watching from the porch, but no one had worked up enough curiosity, or courage, to pry the bodies apart and see if there were any winners. So the bartender summoned the sheriff and the doctor/mortician to the scene.

Jack Huntington was lying directly on top of Deadeye. The sheriff grabbed him by the shoulder and rolled him off. It was hard to see in the semi-darkness so the sheriff asked a couple of the men to help carry the bodies onto the porch. Once there the doctor quickly spotted a blood-soaked circle on Jack's silk embroidered vest just below the third button. A bullet had evidently hit the heart, a lung, or both. He was as dead as a hammer.

Meanwhile, Charlene was kneeling over Deadeye. Tears streamed down her cheeks and dropped gently onto his battered face. Above her sobbing she thought she heard something. A gurgling, grunting noise. And it was coming from Deadeye!

"Rachel, bring me some water," she called. "I think Deadeye may still be alive!" The water arrived in a heartbeat and Charlene took Deadeye's head in her lap and began wiping his face with a damp washcloth. Slowly his moans became louder and in a little while he opened his eyes.

"Charlene," he whispered. "I thought I'd lost ya." Then closing his eyes he lost consciousness.

Charlene asked Clem and Todd to help carry him to her room across the street. For the next two days she did nothing but nurse Deadeye back to health. As soon as he was able to sit up and take nourishment the sheriff came calling.

"Well, Dick, you're a lucky man," smiled the sheriff. "No one has ever tangled with Henry Miles and lived to tell about it."

"What are you talking about?" asked Deadeye. "Who the hell is Henry Miles?"

"That stranger you killed," replied the sheriff. "His real name was Henry Miles, not Jack Huntington. He was wanted in New Mexico and Nevada for murder and extortion. And what's even more interesting is that at one time he had been a U.S. Senator from Indiana and was expelled from Congress for sexual misconduct and racketeering. Yeah, Deadeye, you killed yourself a pretty famous man. Now, what ya gonna do with the reward?"

"What reward, how much?" he stammered as he popped up straighter in bed.

"Oh, 'bout ten thousand dollars" said the sheriff. "Course it will be a few days before you get the money. Looks like you still got some more healing up to do anyway."

The sheriff left, and Deadeye and Charlene began jabbering like a couple of excited chipmunks arguing over an acorn.

News of Deadeye's daring deed soon came to the attention of a writer from Boston. He wrote a glorious account of how the handsome and courageous Deadeye Dick single-handedly took down the notoriously-evil Henry Miles with only his bare hands. A legend was quickly born.

Deadeye and Charlene were married in the spring and bought a small but comfortable cottage outside Silver Springs. Due to his enormous popularity, local politicians urged him to run for state office. Within two years of that fateful night in Horsehead, Deadeye Dick had become a household name, and eventually a three-term governor of a western mining state.

After retiring from politics, Deadeye and Charlene moved to Palm Springs, California. It was there Deadeye met up with Tom Mix and went on to co-star in the silent film classic, *Lazy-Eye Richard and the Stranger From Wolf Canyon*.

Triple F

Brian Snyder glanced at the rear-view mirror. The eighteen-wheeler had cut the distance between them in half and continued to gain ground. His little "rice-burner" got great gas mileage, but lacked get-out-of-the-way power. The best defense was to dart from one lane to another, like a mouse trapped in a room full of ferocious cats.

The cell phone in his pocket vibrated briefly then burst into "Brown-Eyed Girl." It was his wife, Julie. *Why is she calling now? She knows I hate to talk on the phone when I'm driving.* He fumbled with the buttons while keeping one eye on the mirror and one straight ahead.

"Hello, dear. What's up?"

"We've got a problem. There's water all over the floor—and it's getting deeper."

"Where's it coming from?"

"I DON'T KNOW! I'm trying to keep it contained, but I'm running out of towels and blankets."

"Can you shut the water off outside – where it comes into the house?"

"I don't know how to do that! You need to come home. NOW!"

"Okay, okay, I'll turn around at the next exit and get there as quick as I can."

Thoughts bounced in Brian's head like fleas. *Wonder where I put that T-handle for the cut-off valve? I need to call work and tell them I have an emergency at home. Surely a pipe didn't burst? She didn't even say what room it was in. Julie has a tendency to exaggerate. She can turn a drip into a gusher. Maybe it won't be too bad and I can fix it myself.* Plotting a course of action was difficult with limited information.

At home, he discovered finding the T-handle to be elusive. While he dug through every nook and cranny in the garage, laundry room, and storage shed, she followed two steps behind to remind him every nine seconds that the water was getting deeper. His temples began to throb and her panic attack was gas on the fire.

Brian was the kind of guy who liked to combat tense situations with humor. "How high's the water, Mama?" he sang, grinning from ear to ear.

"Deep enough for me to drown you," came the reply. Not exactly the lyric he was looking for, but still, it made him chuckle.

"Did I ever tell you how beautiful you are when you're angry?"

"If that's the case, I should be really pretty by the time *you* get the water shut off. This is *not* funny, Brian. I'm calling a plumber. Right now!"

"Whoa, hold on. Don't get your panties in a wad. There's the T-handle, hiding behind the shovel. Let me get the valve shut off, and we'll try to figure out the problem ourselves."

Brian didn't have a clue where to find the cut-off valve, but figured if he wandered around the yard long enough he'd stumble across it sooner or later. His neighbor, Warren Pierce, a retired Navy officer, came out to retrieve the morning paper and watched Brian zigzag serpentine-fashion about the yard with his head down.

"Looks like you're hot on the trail of something," said Warren. "Is that a snake-charmer you're carrying?"

"No." Brian never looked up. "I'm trying to find the water cut-off. We've got a major leak in the house."

"It's in the same box with the meter." Warren marched to the edge of the yard and pointed to a heavy plastic cover flush with the ground. "Right here."

Brian dug his fingers under the edge of the plastic lid. It wiggled, but would not come free.

"Is there a trick to opening these things?" he asked.

"Not really, but they'll fight ya every inch of the way when you're in a hurry. Push it all the way to one end and pull up."

Brian yanked the lid toward his body and gave a hard jerk. It flew off with a pop, throwing him on his back.

"What's taking so long?" Julie emerged from the garage to find Warren doubled over in laughter and Brian rolling in the grass. "I thought you were going to shut off the valve. Now, I come out here and find you performing doggie tricks for Mr. Pierce. Don't you care that water is ankle deep in our house?"

Warren picked up the T-handle and closed the valve in one smooth motion. "Snyder was rolling on his back in hopes you'd rub his belly, Ma'am."

"I'm not going to rub his belly or scratch behind his ears, but he is getting closer to being in the dog house every minute."

Warren followed them into the house. Two inches of water covered the kitchen floor and several hundred more gallons meandered down the hallway, seeking refuge in the plush carpet of the master bedroom.

"Looks like it may be coming from the water heater." Brian opened the door to a small closet sandwiched between the kitchen and garage. "We're going to have to turn the water back on to pinpoint exactly where the leak is."

"Oh no, you don't," said Julie. "We're calling a plumber. We've got a big enough mess to clean up. I don't need you turning a lake into an ocean."

"It's probably just a busted pipe or bad fitting." Brian wiggled a water line and pointed at various connections like a motorist who doesn't have a clue why the car won't run. "What do you think, Warren?"

"I'm a sailor, Snyder. Not Johnny Fix-it. You'll save yourself time and money by calling somebody who knows what he's doing."

Julie grabbed phone book and fanned to the 'plumbing repair' section of the yellow pages. The first five companies she called were either out of business or unable to make a service call for at least twenty-four hours. Further down the page she noticed a tiny listing for Triple F Plumbing. The business address was on 8th Street, only three blocks away. She was about to hang up when a male voice answered on the tenth ring.

"Yeah," he said, biting off the word.

Julie winced. "Is this . . . Triple F Plumbing?"

"Sure is. What can I do for ya?"

"We have a broken pipe, or something. Water is everywhere. How soon can you have someone over here?"

"That depends. Where are you located?"

"We're at 3214 Persimmon."

"I can have Frank and Fido there in fifteen to twenty minutes. Will that work?"

"Oh, yes. Thank you. It's a red brick home with a yellow Prius out front."

Two hours later a beat up Ford pick-up, with a large F on the door, rumbled into the driveway, sputtered, back-fired, and died. It took another ten minutes for the driver to emerge from the vehicle. He was a short, fat man, who waddled like a duck. A yellow lab followed close behind at a snail's pace. They were both out of breath when they reached the house.

Julie met them in the garage. "You must be Frank," she said, extending her hand.

"No, ma'am, I'm Fido. He's Frank." He pointed to the dog and cracked a Jack-o-lantern smile. "A lot of people get us mixed up. I hear you have a leak. Do you know where the water's coming from?"

"My husband thinks it's somewhere around the water heater, but we're not sure. Come on, I'll show you where it is."

Frank followed the two of them into the house, stuck his nose into the compartment containing the water heater, and barked twice.

Fido pulled a mini flashlight from his shirt pocket and peered into the closet. A labyrinth of copper and steel pipes snaked their way in and around cobwebs and mouse droppings on their way to a dust covered gas water heater. Wrapping his index finger and thumb around the incoming water pipe, he began working his way down, feeling for a split in the copper tubing.

Julie watched him slowly bend at the waist, unaware that she would soon behold the largest and hairiest plumber's crack in recorded history. A massive yawning cavern, so gross and disgusting she couldn't bear to look—yet couldn't turn away.

"I think it's a little lower, keep feeling further down." Brian peeked over Julie's shoulder and wiggled his eyebrows at her. She felt her face flush.

"Yeah, I think I found it. Look right here." Fido pointed the amber beam of his dying flashlight at the drain valve on the water heater. Brian and Julie peered into the semi-darkness.

"See it? Right there. Where the valve screws in." Fido wiggled what was left of the light in the direction of a mysterious gray fixture wearing a white plastic hat.

"Yeah, I think I see it," lied Brian. "How much will it cost to fix?"

"It all depends." Fido straightened and flashed a picket-fence smile. "If it's just the water heater and few fittings, four to five hundred dollars—parts and labor."

Brian winced. *Clean-up was going to be expensive, too. Goodbye week in Jamaica. This water leak was eating their vacation savings faster than a school of piranha at an all-you-can-eat tourist buffet.*

"Oh good," said Julie. "I was afraid it would cost a lot more than that. This is something you can fix today, right?"

"Yes, ma'am. I can go get a new tank while this one is draining. We should have you back in water in a couple of hours."

Julie smiled. "See, Brian," she said in a condescending tone, "how much easier and faster it is when you hire a professional?" She turned to Fido. "Is there someone you'd recommend to clean up this water?"

"I'd use a wet-vac and a carpet shampooer if I were you. The water ain't that deep, and it would save you a lot of money."

"Do we have a wet-vac, Brian?" Julie had no idea what one looked like, but didn't want to appear clueless.

"Uh, no."

"Johnson's Hardware has a fifteen gallon model in their sale paper this week for fifty bucks," said Fido. "That's a good price for one that size—that is, if you want to do the clean-up yourself and save five or six hundred bucks."

"I'll run and get one," said Brian, heading for the door. He was ready for a little fresh air anyway. The entire morning had been a long, stress-filled roller coaster ride. A trip to the hardware store would be a nice reprieve.

Johnson's was a small, family-owned business located in the old part of town. They couldn't compete with the big box-stores on price and inventory, but made up for it with a friendly, knowledgeable staff, exceptional customer service, and free coffee.

It was one of Brian's favorite stores. He could ask questions and get home repair advice in a relaxed atmosphere without feeling like a dummy.

"Good morning, Mr. Snyder." Randal Johnson glanced at his watch. "Well, at least for two more minutes." He smiled. "It's good to see you. What can I help you with?"

"I need a wet-vac. Our plumber said you have one on sale this week."

"We sure do. I've got several to choose from. The one in the circular is this fifteen gallon model over here." They walked to a stack of large boxes near the center of the store. A fully assembled display model was poised atop the stack as if it had just scaled Mount Everest. Brian grabbed the canister and rotated it, inspecting the hose, power cord, and switch. "Looks simple enough to use," he said.

"Are you cleaning up a water spill? I heard you mention a plumber."

"Yeah, water heater went bad. We've got a couple of inches of water in the kitchen floor and down the hall. So far we've been able to keep it out of the rest of the house, but I need to get it sucked up quick."

"Wow, that's a lot of water. You might want to go with a bigger model. Otherwise, you'll be spending more time dumping the canister than vacuuming. Who's your plumber?"

"Some guy named Fido. I think the company is called Triple F. Are you familiar with them?"

"Oh, yeah. I know them well." Johnson grinned. "They have quite a reputation."

"A good one, I hope," said Brian, searching for a grain of confidence. The ear-to-ear grin on Johnson's face created an uneasy feeling in the pit of Brian's stomach.

"It usually takes two or three tries, but they get the job done—eventually. One of our builders refers to Triple F as failures, flops, and fiascos. Most of their business is emergency calls from folks who need someone to come out immediately."

"That would be us," mumbled Brian.

He decided to go with Johnson's recommendation and buy the larger wet-vac. On the way to the check-out counter they passed a display of patio furniture. An eight-foot umbrella caught Brian's eye. *Maybe I should pick up one of these. The closest we're going to get to the beach this year is sitting our lawn chairs in a sandbox next to a kiddie pool.*

Fido's truck was gone, and a garden hose snaked its way from the water heater through the garage to the front yard. Brian opened the wet-vac box and scattered the contents across the driveway. He stabbed the wheels into the bottom of the canister, attached the hose and other parts, occasionally referring to the picture on the carton.

"So that's a wet-vac," said Julie, emerging from the garage. "I thought I heard cursing out here."

"It wasn't cursing. I was just talking to myself."

"It was pretty harsh language for a one-man conversation. You and 'Mr. Fix-it' must have been having quite an argument over how to put this thing together."

Brian wiped the blood from a busted knuckle and tried to ignore her.

"Where do those things go?" Julie pointed to growing pile of leftover parts.

"They throw in a few extra bolts in case you purchase the optional attachments."

"Sure they do." She picked up a clear plastic bag containing a little white booklet. "Hmm, let's see what this says. Step one, discard instruction manual. Step two, fabricate story about leftover parts. Step three, become irritated when your wife . . . ."

Fido's truck sputtered into the driveway, coughed three times, backfired, chopped Julie's sentence in half, and engulfed them in a cloud of carbon monoxide.

"Got you folks a good deal on a water heater." The door flew open and Frank came bouncing out. He was all smiles, wagging his tail and dying to slobber all over the first person who would pat him on the head. Four minutes later, Fido extricated himself from the truck like a sloth emerging from a tar pit.

"I think this one will fit," he said confidently. "It looks about the size of the one you got now." Fido lumbered to the back of the truck and began fooling with the Tommy Lift. "Is there still water coming outta that hose, Mr. Snyder?"

Brian hadn't finished digesting Fido's first two statements, but blindly obeyed the command and chased down the end of the hose. "Not much. Just a drip now and then."

"Good. I'll yank out the old tank and hook up the new one. You folks will be back in water in no time." He flashed his signature grin and wrestled a tall, square box from the tailgate onto a two-wheel dolly. Puffing like the little train that could, he peered over the carton and weaved his way through the garage, knocking over Julie's bicycle and a bucket of red paint whose lid was not on tight. "Oops, sorry about that," he mumbled.

Parking the box near the water heater closet, he returned to the truck to get his tools. His right foot centered the paint spill on the way out and his left one on the way back.

Julie poked Brian in the ribs. "Clean up that spill before he has a chance to roll in it." She wet a rag and began wiping up red footprints leading to the perpetrator. By the time she reached the closet door it looked like a couple of pink elephants had been practicing the two-step on her creamy white, ceramic tile floor.

Fido was staring at the old water heater, rubbing his chin. After much deliberation, he selected a large pipe wrench from his tool box and began to twist fittings above the tank.

Frank came trotting in from the garage to provide supervision. Always the ladies man, he nuzzled Julie's arm and licked her face while she scrubbed tile.

"How long have you had Frank?" she asked.

"He joined the team a couple of weeks after my brother, Fred, passed on," said Fido.

"I'm sorry," said Julie. "Was it difficult dealing with your brother's death?"

"Oh, he didn't die ma'am. He just quit the business. Now he installs satellite dishes. When we started this plumbing company, it was me and Fred and Phil. They wanted to call it Triple F Plumbing, but my given name was Delbert. Since I did most of the fetching, my brothers decided to change my name to Fido. Then, one day, Fred and Phil got into it over who was going to be the CEO and broke up the partnership. Phil was worried we were gonna hafta change the company name. Then, the very next morning this yellow dog showed up. We decided to call him Frank and keep the name Triple F."

"Oh, wow ... uh ... that's a ... fascinating story."

Fido finished unhooking the water lines and attempted to wrestle the water heat from the closet.

"Feels like it hung on something." He wiggled and tugged on the tank again, but it still wouldn't come free. Fishing a small flashlight from his T-shirt pocket, he peered into the closet.

"Damn, this is a gas water heater. Oops, pardon my French, ma'am. I coulda swore it was electric. I'm sorry, but the unit I brought ain't gonna work. I'll hafta take it back and get a gas one. It's after five and my dealer's closed. Will you be all right without water until tomorrow morning?"

Julie rose from her knees, glared into his eyes, and shook her paint-soaked rag in his face. "Whadda you mean it won't work? You're supposed to be a professional plumber. That's why I called you. A *professional* would know the difference between gas and electric."

"I'm sorry, ma'am. I do know the difference, but I must've loaded the wrong box by mistake," Fido pleaded with his best whipped-puppy impression. "I'll have the right one here *first thing* in the morning. I promise."

Brian heard Julie's voice grow louder and more threatening. He abandoned the paint spill in the garage and hurried to the scene of the commotion. "What's going on?"

"Mr. Plumber here brought the wrong water heater," said Julie. "Now, we're not going to have any running water till sometime tomorrow. No shower, no washing your hands, and no flushing the toilet. Does that about cover it, Mr. Plumber?"

"Well, you won't be able to do laundry, run the dishwasher, or water your lawn either," said Fido, staring at his shoes.

"Oh my God," declared Julie. "I don't know whether to laugh or cry."

"I sincerely apologize, ma'am." Fido inched toward the garage, never turning his back on his attacker. "It was an honest mistake. They open at seven-thirty. I'll swap this one out and be here by eight." He slipped the two-wheeler under the box and hustled it back to the truck, displaying more energy in thirty seconds than he would normally exert in an eight hour day.

The steam spewing out of Julie's ears slowed to a fizzle, but her scowl remained. Frank hid under the truck while Fido loaded the box, then the two of them shot out of the driveway like bank robbers fleeing a hold-up gone awry.

Brian and Julie spent the next two hours sucking water with the shop vac, moving furniture, and mopping up as much residual moisture as the laws of physics would allow. Brian set up a couple of box fans to help dry the house while Julie wrung out the water-soaked bath towels she'd employed as levees to control the flood.

"I'm exhausted." Brian wilted into a kitchen chair. "And starving. Why don't we go out and eat?"

"I can't go out in public looking like this. My hair's a mess and I've been sweating like a water buffalo." Julie opened her hands and examined the paint-stained fingers, dyed pink from cleaning up Fido's footprints. "Why don't you just go pick something up—or order a pizza?"

"I was craving Mexican. We could go to that dumpy little joint where the lighting is so dim you can barely see your plate. No one would recognize us there and the smell of searing animal flesh on the fajita skillets would hide our odor."

"Forget it, Brian. I'm not going. It's take out or a pizza, your choice."

"All right, pizza it is. I'll call in the order and you can run over to Mr. Pierce's house and wash up while we're waiting." Brian wiggled his eyebrows and grinned at Julie. "Better hurry or the pizza boy will catch you red-handed."

The alarm went off at a quarter to six. Brian rolled over and slapped the snooze button. That would buy ten minutes before the annoying DJ at KLXR would remind him it was time to get out of bed and face the world. Seven minutes later it went off again.

"It's Friday the thirteenth." The DJ's voice was giddy with excitement. "For all of you named Jason, it's time to put on your hockey mask and head to work. If you're somebody else, just wear that zombie face you keep in the closet next to those double-knit plaid pants Aunt Polly gave you for Christmas."

Brian turned off the radio, rolled out of bed, and staggered to the kitchen for some coffee. He picked up the pot and reached for the faucet. That's when it hit him. No water. There would be no coffee, no shower, and no peace in this house until a new water heater was installed and things were back to normal.

He tip-toed into the bedroom and picked out some clothes for work. His contingency plan would be to stop at the convenience store for coffee and a biscuit, then swing by the gym, fake a five minute workout and take a quick shower.

"Are you going in early?" Julie rolled over in bed and faced the closet.

"Yeah, I thought I would," said Brian. "Missing yesterday put me behind. You and the plumber can handle replacing the water heater without me, can't you?"

"I suppose so. Hopefully, he'll be in and out by noon. Is the coffee ready?"

Brian bit his lip. "No, dear." He paused. "We don't have any water."

"Oh, so that's why you're slipping out so early. I forgot about the water." She punched her pillow, inhaled deeply, and let out a sigh that made the curtains quiver. "Enjoy your coffee and donuts. And don't worry about me and Fido. We'll be fine—just fine."

At eleven minutes after nine Fido's truck sputtered into the driveway. It made a horrible gagging sound before it died like a wino with dry-heaves. After the cloud of exhaust fumes lifted, the door screeched open, and Fido and Frank emerged. Julie and Mr. Pierce were camped out in lawn chairs just inside the garage doorway. He'd brought over a pot of coffee to help calm Julie's nerves.

"Where've you been?" demanded Julie. "I've been expecting you for over an hour. What happened to first thing in the morning?"

"I got caught in school traffic," said Fido. "Then Frank and I got separated at the plumbing warehouse. Every time I went up one aisle, he came down another. We like to never found the right water heater. When we finally got loaded up and headed over here, the fuel light came on, and I had to stop for gas."

"Is that all you filled up on?" asked Julie. "Those white flakes on your shirt look like donut glaze. Did you stop by the coffee shop too?"

"Only for a minute." Fido flashed a red-faced grin. "Frank won't let me drive past without stopping. He's crazy about their scones."

"Well, we can't let a little thing like the Snyder's water problems get between Frank and his scones, now, can we?" The sarcasm flew over Fido's head like a jumbo jet crossing the vast wasteland of the Sahara Desert.

"No, ma'am. He loves them scones." Fido chuckled and patted Frank on the head.

"Would you like some help getting the water heater in the house?" asked Mr. Pierce. He sensed Julie's irritation rising from a simmer to a boil. Poor Fido was already in hot water, and she would scald and pluck him like a Sunday chicken if he didn't get to work soon.

"It's easy to unload with the Tommy Lift," said Fido, "but if you could make sure I've got a clear path to the closet door, I'd sure appreciate it." He walked to the back of the truck and lowered the box and dolly onto the driveway. By the time he headed to the house, Julie and Mr. Pierce had created a six-lane expressway through the garage.

Fido dropped the box with a thud. Putting his hands on his knees, he puffed and panted as if he'd carried a refrigerator on his back across an alligator-filled sewage ditch. After several deep breaths, he straightened up, tugged at the waistband of his pants and said, "I guess I'll go find the meter and shut off the gas."

Frank wedged his way between Fido and open closet door. He peered inside, lifted his right front leg, stiffened his tail, and whimpered twice. Mr. Pierce leaned forward to see what had caught Frank's attention.

"Uh . . . Mr. Fido, I'm not a plumber, but it seems your partner has spotted something on one of these pipes that looks a lot like a shut-off valve."

Fido fished a miniature flashlight from his shirt pocket and waved the beam in front of Frank's outstretched nose. "Well, I'll be darn. Good job, Frank." He reached down and patted the dog. "That'll make life a whole lot easier." Fido closed the valve and disconnected the flexible pipe from the water heater. Leaning into the closet he wrapped his arms around the tank in a bear hug and with a series of grunts, groans, and a select string of magical cuss words, wrestled it into the hallway.

The new water heater slid into place without any trouble. In a matter of minutes, he had the water lines connected and vent pipe in place. The tank was ready to be filled. "Humph, wonder why I didn't see that yesterday?" Fido cocked his head to the right and slapped the left side with an open palm, as if something was lodged in his brain and he was trying to knock it out through his ear.

"What is it?" asked Julie. "Is something wrong?"

"Oh no, ma'am. I just found a cut-off valve on the incoming water line."

"What does that mean?"

"If we'd have found this yesterday, and closed the valve, you could've had water to the rest of the house while the tank was being replaced. Cold only, mind you, but plenty for drinking and flushing the stool."

Julie's jaw fell open in amazement. She looked Fido in the eye, shook her head slowly from side to side, and exhaled like a deflating balloon. Turning to Mr. Pierce, she rolled her eyes, bit her lower lip, and stomped off in search of fresh air.

Fido turned the water on at the meter, while Frank checked for leaks. He let out a couple of short whimpers and raised a paw to indicate a slow drip at one of the connections. Fido selected a crescent wrench to tighten the fitting. Mr. Pierce held his breath. Frank closed his eyes and panted (sending up a doggie prayer). With the tactical expertise of a bomb squad technician, Fido exhaled slowly, leaned on the wrench, and gave the fitting a quarter turn. The drip stopped. Neighbors reported hearing a collective sigh three blocks away.

"That was easy," said Fido, drops of sweat still racing from his forehead to his chin. "We're in the home stretch now."

He grabbed the flexible gas line and tried to connect it to the new water heater. It was too short. He pulled, cursed, tugged, and twisted the line trying to milk a few more centimeters of length from the crinkled tubing. After a battle of epic proportions lasting a full minute and a half, his shoulders sagged into the collapse of defeat.

"Dang, we were so close. If the tank had been rotated two inches to the left it would've lined up perfectly. Frank, you were supposed to check that before we turned on the water." The lab buried his muzzle in his chest and threw a paw over the bridge of his nose.

"Too late now," said Fido. "Let's see if we got a longer pipe in the truck." Frank took off in a trot with Fido lumbering behind like a tortoise responding to a house fire.

Julie rejoined Mr. Pierce in the doorway of the garage. "Are they finished?"

"No," said Pierce. "The gas line wouldn't reach. They're looking for a longer one."

The rattle of metal objects being shuffled and banged about in the back of the truck continued for several minutes. It ended with a sharp yelp from Frank and a couple of choice expletives from Fido.

"Need to clean the back of that truck out one of these days." Fido was panting louder than Frank by the time he covered the thirty feet between the back of the pick-up and garage. "You can find everything in there (puff, puff, pant) 'cept what you're looking for. The ones with the right fittings are too short and the ones that are long enough have the wrong fittings. I'm going to have to run to Plumber's Supply and pick one up."

Julie groaned, looked to the heavens and shook her head.

"I'll be back in about half an hour," said Fido, waddling toward the truck. With every step his pants crept further down his backside. Julie turned her head to avoid further retinal damage and looked at her watch. It read eleven-fifteen.

"Let's get some lunch," said Mr. Pierce. "My treat. I have a feeling we have plenty of time before Fido returns."

Julie released her first smile of the day. "We could tour the Great Wall of China too."

After lunch, Mr. Pierce returned to his lawn and pretended to work in a flower bed. He was old school and of the opinion that a gentleman didn't leave a woman alone in the company of repairmen, even those as hapless as Fido.

At precisely 14:46 military time, Mr. Pierce spotted the Triple F truck turning the corner onto Persimmon Drive. Frank was hanging out the passenger window, tongue flapping in the breeze like a matador's cape at a bullfight.

Fido steered the rattletrap into the Synder's driveway and shut off the engine. He remained in the cab for several minutes, head down and body wiggling like a five-year-old putting the finishing touches on a Crayola masterpiece for his mom to display on the refrigerator.

He muttered something audible only to Frank before the two of them rolled out of the truck and sauntered into the garage. Julie met him at the back door.

"Well, the prodigal son has finally returned," she said. "I was going to time you, but I only have a thirteen month calendar. Did you and Frank have a nice siesta after lunch?"

Fido's face broke into a picket fence grin. "Ma'am, you must be one of them psychotics. It's hard to stay awake after a couple of burgers. Me and Frank was just gonna rest our eyes a couple of minutes and when we woke up it was two hours later."

"I think you mean psychic," said Pierce, coming up behind Fido. "Do you really think Mrs. Synder can predict the future?"

"I don't know, but she called that one right. Let me get this pipe on and I predict she'll have hot water in a very short time."

Fido removed the short pipe, applied Teflon tape to the bare fittings, and attached the new pipe, busting only one knuckle. He opened the valve, held the start button down, and lit the pilot. A full minute later he released the button and bent over to get a better view of the burner.

"Something ain't right with the flame." His pants and underwear once again receded down his backside like waves at low tide. "Maybe I can fine tune it." He adjusted his crescent wrench to a smaller gap and began twisting up and down on a brass coupling then opened and closed the air intake. Nothing worked.

"I bet it's set-up for propane instead of natural gas." Fido scrambled to his feet. "There should be another orifice with the owner's manual." He turned the shipping box upside down and shook out a clear plastic bag labeled 'choke hazard.' Tearing open the package, he dumped the contents onto the garage floor.

"There it is." He picked up a miniature zip-lock bag and waved it in front of Julie and Mr. Pierce. The part was so small Julie had to squint to see it.

"That tiny thing will fix the problem?" she asked.

"Yes, ma'am. Right now it's getting too much gas." Fido dropped to his knees, closed the valve on the gas line, and disassembled the coupler to remove the propane orifice. He gave the line a jiggle, and the offending part fell into his hand. Swapping it for the one in the zip-lock bag, he attempted to insert the new orifice into the housing.

"Dang," he muttered. "I dropped it." Picking up his flashlight, he surveyed the cemetery of dust bunnies and mouse droppings that covered the closet floor.

"There it is," he said, with the enthusiasm of a nine-year-old on an Easter egg hunt. He tried to pick the orifice up, but it squirted away from the pinches of his bratwurst-size finger and thumb. Time after time, the tiny piece dodged left and right to avoid capture. Julie and Mr. Pierce peeked over Fido's shoulder to watch the game of fat cat and elusive mouse.

"Aha, I've got you now." The trembling orifice lay naked and alone next to a water pipe coming up through the floor. Pierce began humming the theme from *Jaws* as Fido moved in on his prey like a sloth wading through molasses. With a quick stab, he pinned the orifice to the floor. Rolling it between his finger and thumb, he gave a little squeeze. It shot from his grasp and into the gap between the pipe and floor.

"SHIT!" screamed Fido. Before he could stop, he had rattled off a string of expletives that even a thirty-year Navy man like Mr. Pierce had never heard.

"Oh, no," Julie groaned. She tilted back her head and closed her eyes.

"Do you have a magnet in your truck?" asked Pierce. "Maybe you can go through the crawl hole and find it that way."

"It'd have to be a pretty big crawl hole, Mr. Pierce," said Fido. "Besides, I'm claustrophobic. It'll be faster just to pick up another one from the parts store."

"Nothing you do is fast," said Julie. "This has gone on far too long. I'm calling your boss and getting someone over here who can fix this thing once and for all."

"Now, ma'am, don't get all excited," pleaded Fido. "You don't want to call Phil. He gets all worked up over this kind of stuff."

"HE gets worked up?" Julie's voice climbed two octaves. "What about me? You should be worried about how *your customer* feels." She stomped into the kitchen and began punching in numbers on a cordless phone.

"Yeah," came a voice on the other end. "What can I do for ya?"

"This is Julie Snyder. Fido's been here two and a half days, and we don't have hot water yet. Send someone over who can get the job done NOW, or I'm going to call the Better Business Bureau and file a complaint."

"Hold your horses, ma'am. I'll be over in a few minutes and take care of it personally. Put Fido on the line, will ya. I need to find where he screwed up before I can fix it." Julie stepped into the garage and handed the phone to Fido.

Julie and Mr. Pierce couldn't make out the words, but the tone of the voice coming through the receiver was loud and clear. Fido grimaced and moved the phone further from his ear.

"I was replacing the orifice, and the new one fell into a crack and went under the house. We need one for natural gas. Could you pick one up on your way over?" More sharp barks shot from the receiver.

"Okay, me and Frank will be waiting." Fido handled Julie the phone and headed toward his truck.

Julie's next call was to Brian.

"I need you to come home NOW. This so-called plumber screws up everything he touches. I've called his boss, and he's on his way over—claims he can fix it. You need to be here to make sure it gets done right."

"But, honey, I can't just up and leave. We've got a meeting with an important client in a few minutes. How am I going to explain this to the boss?"

"Tell him you have a family emergency. Make something up—I don't care. Just get here as soon as you can." Julie hung up before he could argue further.

Brian hung his head and sighed. He found his boss, Carlton Fitzhugh, shuffling through a stack of file folders in preparation for the meeting. The news was not well received.

"Snyder, you have more family emergencies than the entire State of Georgia. It seems every time we have an important meeting scheduled you find some way to skip out. This is twice in one week. If you keep missing, pretty soon we'll figure out how to do things without you."

"I'm sorry, Mr. Fitzhugh." Brian felt the knot tighten in his stomach. "This will be the last time. I'll make sure of that." He turned and headed for the parking lot. *What an asshole* played like a broken record inside his head all the way home.

Fido's truck was still parked in front of the garage when he arrived.

Fifteen minutes later a silver BMW convertible eased into the driveway. A tall, slender man emerged. The rays of the late-afternoon sun darted between the gelled waves of his jet-black hair. After extolling a few unpleasantries on Fido, he strolled into the garage, his after-shave preceding him by a good twelve feet.

"Good afternoon, Mr. and Mrs. Snyder," he said, extending his hand. "I'm Phil. I apologize for any inconvenience we may have caused you in the delay of this repair." He flashed a sly smile beneath a thin, handlebar moustache. Reaching into the pocket of his freshly pressed white shirt, he produced a tiny bag containing an orifice. "I'll have this installed in a couple of minutes, and you'll be back in business."

Mr. Pierce walked over to Fido. "So you and Phil are brothers? I don't see much family resemblance."

"Yeah, Dad used to say that, too." Fido chuckled. "But Mom would always tell him Phil got his looks from her side of the family and I got my brains from his."

"I see," said Pierce. "Well, that makes sense . . . I guess."

Phil pulled a red bandana from his back pocket and spread it front of the water heater. Kneeling on the bandana, he inserted the new part into the coupling and tightened the fittings. A minute later, he opened the gas valve and lit the pilot. When the burner kicked on, he dialed the air intake until the flame reached a perfect shade of blue.

"There you go folks." Phil rose to his feet, folded the bandana and returned it to his hip pocket. "Fido should have your invoice tallied up by now. You can write him a check or give us a credit card number. We're easy to do business with."

Julie bit her lip to keep from laughing.

"If there's anything else I can do for you ma'am, just give me a call." Phil stared into her sea-green eyes and wiggled his eyebrows ever so slightly. A gold tooth sparkled in the center of his Snidely-Whiplash-smile.

"Thank you very much," said Brian, stepping between them. "We're glad to finally have this behind us. Hopefully, it won't give us any more trouble."

"The water heater has a manufacturer's warranty and we guarantee our labor for thirty days. If it gives you any problems let me know and we'll take care of it." Phil threw back his shoulders and strolled toward the BMW, keeping one eye on Julie.

Fido and Frank waited until Phil got out of sight before waddling up the driveway to present the invoice. Frank had the folded, yellow piece of paper crossways in his mouth with an ample amount of drool coating each side. He dropped it gently in front of Julie and pushed it forward with his nose.

"You pick it up," she told Brian.

He searched for a dry spot, then decided to use a BBQ spatula from the garage wall. Wiping it off on a paint rag, he unfolded the invoice and strained to read the blurred number on the bottom line.

"Seven hundred and twenty-eight dollars?" Brian's jaw reached for his chest.

"Yeah, I was kinda surprised it was so low myself," said Fido. "After Phil got done chewing me out, he told me to take two hundred off your bill for keeping you out of water so long."

"Gee, thanks," said Julie. "Not only are you slow, but you're expensive too."

"You must have seen that on the back of my truck." Fido grinned. "Some folks don't think it's a very catchy slogan, but I can see you've got a good sense of humor."

Julie went in the house and returned in a few minutes with a check. "Here you go, Mr. Fido. This ought to cover the next payment on Phil's BMW with enough left over to buy Frank a chew toy."

"Thank you, ma'am. Frank appreciates tips." The yellow lab rose on his back legs and rested his front paws on Julie's hips. He looked up at her and whined like he was trying to speak.

"He wants to give you a kiss," said Fido.

"How about a scratch behind the ears instead?" Julie stroked her fingers up and down behind the dog's head while drool trickled from both sides of his mouth, coating her flip-flops.

"Time to go, Frank," said Fido. The dog applied a thick layer of slobber to both of Julie's hands before dropping to all fours and trotting toward the truck. Fido closed the tailgate and they headed down the street. The yellow words printed on the back of his truck stood out against a blue background. *We're Slow, but We're Expensive.*

Two weeks later Fitzhugh called Brian into his office.

"Snyder, the wife wants a shower installed in our pool house. Do you know a good plumber you'd recommend for the job?"

The corners of Brian's mouth curled in a devilish smile.

Meet Rachel Crofton

Another author was reading my work one day and remarked, "Russell, you write like a girl." A man less secure about being in touch with his feminine side might have been offended by such a remark. Not me. I just scrunched my eyebrows, shot back an icy stare, and shouted, "Oh, yeah?"

The truth is a lot of best-selling authors have feminine names. Are they all women? I don't know, but if somebody wants to offer this Rachel Crofton a million dollar advance for her next novel, all I can say is, "Where do we sign?"

Peeves I Like to Pet

Peeves make wonderful pets. You can take them anywhere. They don't require food, water, or vaccinations, although I do recommend grooming them from time to time.

One of my favorite things about peeves is that you can have as many as you want. In fact, I have an entire kennel of them. Peeves love attention and like to come out for a playful romp at every available opportunity. Like other pets, regular exercise is essential to keeping them healthy and happy.

Hurry Up and Wait is one of my favorites. She likes to sit on the counter while I fix my hair and apply make-up. In the other room, my husband, Brad, is pacing like a lion that just had its kill taken over by a pack of hyenas. How that man can watch a motionless fishing rod for two hours, or sit on a rock in the woods for half a day without seeing anything, is beyond me. But tell him you need five minutes to get ready, and you'd think you were asking Richard Nixon to surrender the Watergate tapes.

I tell him, "Good things come to those who wait."

Running on Empty is another of my high achievers. I hate pumping gas. The wind messes with my hair, my ankles freeze, and the scent of gasoline lingers on my hands for days. If there's enough in the tank to get from point "A" to point "B," that's all you need, right?

There's a little icon on the dash that indicates when the tank is almost empty. I don't pay a whole lot of attention to it, but the flashing red light seems to really annoy Brad. He immediately flies into a tirade about how we're going to be late, followed by an extended period of prayer in which he asks for the fumes to hold out till we get to the nearest station.

I really think he should plan better and allow more time, but the last time I mentioned it he glared at me with fiery eyes and clenched teeth. He doesn't take suggestions well when he's pushing a car in the rain.

Caring for pets is a good way for a child to learn responsibility. Our son, Cain, was only four when he adopted "Leave the Light On."

The poor little peeve was a gift from an elderly couple, and appeared scrawny and malnourished when Cain first brought him home. How some people can be so cruel as to starve a pet is beyond me. If you can't afford to feed a peeve you shouldn't get one to start with.

It was so cute to watch the two of them play. They ran from room to room, Cain stretching on tippy-toes to turn on every light in the house. Bedrooms, bathrooms, closets, microwave ovens, it didn't matter. Bulbs were made to shine, and shine they did.

Our electric meter spun like a roulette wheel on steroids. Unfortunately, it always landed on red. When Brad saw the amount of the bank drafts he blew a fuse. Surely there was a mistake. How could there be that many digits to the left of a decimal point?

After a brief – but heated – family meeting, it was decided "Leave the Lights On" had to go. Brad gave Cain two weeks to find the peeve a new home. I put an ad on craigslist offering a friendly, loving, house-broken pet for only twenty dollars.

The president of a motel chain saw my ad and dispatched some fellow named Tom to pick up the peeve. From what I hear, it's worked out well for both of them. Tom and "Leave the Lights On" have become virtually inseparable.

I just love happy endings, don't you?

Raising Cain

It was Brad's idea to name the baby Cain. At first, Rachel resisted. That name had always been associated with trouble and it didn't seem fair to bring a child into this world with a millstone hanging around his neck. But, after twenty-six hours of labor, she was ready to change her mind.

The doctor had been coming in every two hours to check her progress. He would examine her to see how the baby was turned, if it had dropped down properly, all that good stuff. He kept glancing at his watch and frowning. The 8 am Saturday tee-time his pharmaceutical salesman buddy had booked for them was in serious jeopardy.

Brad brought Rachel to the hospital when the contractions first began at 6 am on Friday. They were both excited and anxious to meet their little bundle of joy and put nine months of pregnancy behind them. The pains started as a minor inconvenience. Brad held her hand and coached her through the breathing techniques they had been taught in Lamaze class. This wasn't so bad. Everything was going according to plan.

Then weird things begin to happen. Time ground to a halt. An hour took days, sometimes months, to pass. The pains became frequent and more intense. Sharp stabbing sensations in Rachel's lower abdomen forced her to scream, curse, and look for someone to choke. She grabbed her loving coach by the collar and twisted till his face turned blue.

"You're the cause of this, you son-of-a-bitch," she hissed. "You planted this evil seed in my belly." Brad's eyes bulged in horror when she ripped the crucifix from around his neck and threw it across the room.

Both Grandmas-to-be glanced at the expectant parents and went on yakking. Like a couple of old soldiers, they compared battle scars from their child-bearing days. They had come to "be there for them," and witness the "blessed event." Their stories did nothing to ease Rachel's pain. This hurt like hell, and she wanted to get it over with.

The baby refused to put his head down and get in proper position. This had been a difficult pregnancy from the beginning. The little unborn demon was determined to fight every step of the way.

Between contractions, Brad overheard the doctor talking on his cell phone in the hall. "This one's going to take a while, Barney. You guys start without me. I'll catch up on the back nine."

By 7 am Saturday, Rachel was physically and emotionally drained. Her hair stuck out in every direction and the bags under her eyes had grown into suitcases. Brad's mother had the poor taste to take photos of her daughter-in-law in hard labor. When contractions hit, Rachel's eyes would bulge, and unnatural growls sprang from behind clenched teeth. Too bad she couldn't spew green bile.

After the choking incident, Brad stayed out of arm's reach. He cowered behind the recliner every time she started chugging like a locomotive.

The veteran nursing staff used every trick in their arsenal to get the baby to rotate. Rachel was near the end of her rope, and more importantly, the good doctor was late for his appointment with Barney. If the baby wouldn't come out on his own, then by golly, it was time to go in there and drag him out.

"Mrs. Crofton, I think it's time to consider a caesarean. This will be a bikini cut," he said, drawing an imaginary line just above her pubic hair with his finger. "You'll be able to wear a two-piece swimsuit without the scar showing. Are you okay with that?"

She nodded and groaned a weak, "Uh-huh." *Put a metal zipper from top to bottom, for all I care.* How she would look in a bikini was the last thing on her mind.

The medical staff unhooked the various monitors used to track the baby's vitals and whisked the gurney down the hall to an operating room. Brad appeared a few minutes later wearing disposable scrubs, hairnet, and a mask.

"Wanna play doctor?" he asked, from a safe distance.

Rachel forced a weak smile. *If Dr. Frankenstein could reach you, she'd replace your brain with one that worked.*

The doctor arrived and assured her the procedure wasn't going to hurt. Finally! After twenty-six hours of experiencing every level of pain known to motherhood, they were going to expose her to something that wouldn't hurt? Why did they wait so damn long?

He raked a dull scalpel across her lower belly a couple times, popped her open like a ripe watermelon, and reached in to remove the cause of discomfort.

Cain was covered with an icky slime. His large head and purplish-pink body reminded Rachel of the alien in ET. The doctor held him up like a trophy. "Congratulations, Mrs. Crofton. Would you like to hold your son?"

Rachel took the baby in her arms and tried to cuddle him. He screamed like a banshee and kicked like a bucking bronco. All his working parts were in perfect condition, with the exception of attitude. It was the beginning of a love/hate relationship for both of them.

Rachel's mother stayed with the couple for a week after the birth. Cain didn't respond well to her either. He had an insatiable appetite, but refused to sleep. The three of them took shifts catering to his demands. No one got any rest due to the constant crying and screaming. Brad tried to calm Rachel, but she wasn't having it. "I just had a baby, damn it. Give me a break."

Grandma Crofton was a real trooper. But by the end of the week, sleep deprivation caught up with her and she wandered through the house like a zombie. When Brad's father came to pick her up, she got a sudden burst of energy and practically ran to the car. That left just Brad and Rachel to care for the little hellion and adjust to their "new life" as parents.

Young couples are told repeatedly that having a baby will change your life. What life? They no longer had one. After a few days, Brad returned to work and left Rachel trapped in a 1,500-square-foot prison with a little dictator controlling her every move.

People kept saying, "It gets easier as they get older." Those people are either delusional or suffer from some form of memory loss. Each time Cain showed improvement in one area, such as sleeping through the night or using the potty, he'd find two new ways to torture or scare the hell out of his parents.

If Rachel hadn't seen the doctor pull him from her belly, she would have sworn the hospital switched babies. Cain bore no resemblance, physical or behavioral, to her or Brad. He was loud, obnoxious, and unruly. His father and mother are quiet, reserved, and easy going. It just didn't make sense.

Then one day Brad's mother came to visit. Camilla Throckmorton (or Cruella, Rachel's pet name for her mother-in-law) lived five hours away. You can find a picture of her by typing "two-faced" at Wikipedia.com.

When Brad and Rachel announced their engagement, Camilla smiled, hugged Rachel and proclaimed, "You'll be the daughter I never had." Then she spent the next three months begging Brad to break off the engagement. Why would her precious boy want to travel coach when he should be flying first-class? She cried non-stop at the wedding. One of the groomsmen bet the best man $100 that Camilla would stand up and tell the preacher why the couple shouldn't be joined in holy matrimony, but she just sat there, dressed in black, sobbing into a handkerchief.

After Cain learned to walk, Camilla began referring to him as her "little man," and instructed him to address her as Grand-Mother, as if it were two words. They got along splendidly. Watching them interact made Rachel's stomach churn. The fruit of her womb had inherited the personality traits of a Witch from Hell.

The thought of Cain growing up to be like Camilla made Rachel physically ill. She contemplated suicide for a couple of days. The only thing that kept her going was the vain hope that she might be a positive influence on the child.

The Croftons enrolled Cain in pre-school shortly after his third birthday. Brad thought it would be good for him to be around other children, learn to share, develop social skills, that sort of stuff. It was a half-day class and would give Rachel some free time to run errands and work on regaining her sanity.

Two weeks into the program she got a call from the school administrator. "Mrs. Crofton, we'd like to schedule a conference with you and your husband to discuss Cain's behavior."

"What happened?" Rachel asked. "Did he bite someone, or pull a little girl's hair?"

"Oh, no, nothing like that. We'll talk about it when you come in."

She refused to provide any details, just provided a date and time to be there and hung up the phone.

Over the next fifteen years Brad and Rachel attended hundreds of counseling sessions. It didn't take long to figure out the school's strategy. They intentionally withhold information so they can blind-side defenseless parents. It's the old deer-in-the-headlights tactic. Bewildered moms and dads sit there bug-eyed with their chins on their chests while being told their child needs prescription drugs to control his outrageous behavior.

Cain did not have a problem getting along with other children. Quite the contrary, he displayed extraordinary leadership and organizational skills. In a short time, he had managed to convince his classmates they were being mistreated to the point of abuse. He appointed commanders to govern the rank and file, and laid out a strategic plan to force the administration to comply with their demands. Shorter naps, a complete revision of the school lunch menu, and increased play time topped their list. Cain also felt the curriculum should focus on the liberal arts rather than ABCs and counting to ten.

Rachel couldn't believe her ears. "My three-year-old is being expelled from pre-school for organizing a mutiny?" Cain sat between his mom and dad while Ms. Ralston read the charges. He looked so innocent.

"Mommy, is Ms. Ralston mad at me? Did I do something wrong?" Alligator tears crawled down his tiny cheeks and passed a trembling lower lip.

Rachel had never been nominated for Mother-of-the-Year, but a certain maternal instinct kicks in when someone attacks a woman's baby.

"What kind of school is this?" she asked. "You're supposed to be controlling the students instead of the other way around. If the kids are misbehaving, try some corrective disciplinary action. Don't just throw them out on their ear."

Rachel's free afternoons were in serious jeopardy. Somehow, she had to make them reconsider expulsion.

"Now, now, Mrs. Crofton, let's not get upset. Cain is a wonderful child. It's just that he's so . . . so . . . unusually gifted." Ms. Ralston smiled, pleased with her tactful response.

Rachel smiled back. *She's given me an opening. What an idiot.*

"Why, thank you, Ms. Ralston. Brad and I realize that Cain is not a perfect child. That's one of the reasons we chose Presidential Academy. You have a reputation for molding and developing young minds. We want that for our son. Won't you please give him another chance?"

Cain leaned forward in his chair, cocked his little head, and squeezed out a few more tears. "Pleeease . . . Ms. Ralston. I promise I'll be good." It was a performance worthy of an Oscar nomination.

"Well . . . all right. We'll make an exception this time, but from now on, Cain, you must obey the rules and do what your teacher tells you. No more stirring up trouble. Do you understand?"

"Yes, Ma'am." He bounced off his chair and ran around the desk to give her a hug. That sealed the deal. The boy was learning more than academics.

By the time Cain started the fourth grade, he had mastered most of the scheming, manipulative traits that would become his trademark. Classmates who came for a sleepover were conned into doing chores. For the small sum of five dollars they could purchase the privilege of mowing the lawn. Folding laundry cost two dollars, and if Cain was in a really charitable mood, his friends could wash the Crofton's dishes for free.

He was handsome, funny, and intelligent. Adults were captivated by his magnetic personality and charming demeanor. Peers performed dangerous feats and outrageous pranks in hopes of gaining his approval. Everyone wanted to be a member of the Cain Crofton fan club.

The first two weeks of July were reserved for Grand-Mother. Cain loved her dearly and looked forward to their time together. She never took him to amusement parks, sporting events, or the zoo. Time was too precious to waste on such foolishness. Her annual "boot camp" taught the finer points of taking advantage of your fellow man.

Camilla Throckmorton had been married five times. The first one, she'd be quick to tell you, was her only mistake in life. She was young and naïve when she met and fell in love with Alan Crofton. True love may have some redeeming value, but it takes money and prestige to open doors beyond the reach of hard-working middle-class men and women. By the time she figured out they were on the road to Nowheresville, Brad had been born.

She resented the fact that Alan's meager salary could not support her high-maintenance needs. He even had the gall to suggest that *she* get a job. They fought like cats and dogs. Money, or lack thereof, was at the center of every argument. Alan foolishly believed that it should be spent paying the mortgage, utilities and groceries. Camilla fought fiercely for high-priority expenses such as new clothing, manicures, pedicures, and the hottest hair styles in Hollywood. One simply could not go out in public without being well-groomed and properly dressed.

Finally, just to shut him up, she agreed to look for a job. She secured an interview for a secretarial position with the most reputable law firm in town. To prove her point about being properly dressed, she wore her shortest skirt, six-inch pumps, and a silk blouse with a plunging neckline.

William McMaster, a distinguished-looking gentleman in his early fifties, and senior partner of the law firm, conducted the interview. Camilla watched the reflection of her long slender legs in McMasters bifocals as she repeatedly crisscrossed them during the preliminary small-talk leading up the interview's lone question.

"When can you start?" McMasters smiled. "I can see you'll be a real asset to our firm."

The firm's junior partner, Kyle Penders, was appreciative of Camilla's assets as well. Penders was an up-and-comer, only two years out of law school, flawlessly handsome and full of self-confidence. He was charming, convincing, and a man with absolutely no moral or ethical compass. Lies dripped from both corners of his mouth.

Camilla fell madly in love. Kyle was the kind of man that could take her places. She fantasized that their sordid affair would lead to wedded bliss and a happily-ever-after storybook ending. But first they needed to get rid of a couple of pieces of baggage, namely Alan and that blonde bimbo Kyle called his wife.

The divorce proceedings went exactly as she had planned. Alan was clueless to the wicked ways of the world. When Camilla blamed him for breaking up their happy home, he wilted like a wet newspaper and agreed to all her demands. After all, she told him, a *good* father would do what was best for Brad.

Her lawyer (Kyle Penders, of course) convinced the judge to award her the house, full custody of the baby, child support, and a healthy dose of alimony.

Now, if she could just get Penders to dump the bimbo. That was easier said than done. He lied, stalled, and procrastinated, dragging the affair on for a couple more years. She eventually got past her denial and accepted the fact that Kyle was never going to pay for free milk as long as she played the proverbial cow. It was time to look for greener pastures.

Over the next fifteen years, Camilla married and divorced three more times. Each man was wealthier than the one before. When the time came to split, the legal knowledge and experience gained at the firm served her well. Relieving ex-husbands of an over-abundance of wealth was just Camilla's way of stimulating the economy.

Young Brad was shuffled from one private school to another while his mother bilked millionaires and cultivated social status. She would "send for him" on holidays or special occasions when she wanted to parade him around like a prize pup at the Westminster Dog Show.

On the fourth anniversary of Camilla's thirty-ninth birthday, she finally caught the "Big Fish." Andrew Throckmorton was forty years her senior and one of the ten richest men in the world. His children despised Camilla and tried to convince their father she was a gold-digger. He would not be dissuaded. All his buddies at 'The Club' had trophy wives, and by God, he deserved one too.

One of the things Camilla found attractive about Throckmorton, in addition to money, was his exceedingly poor health. It's not every day you get a chance to marry a billionaire who already has one foot in the grave. Andrew had been diagnosed with congestive heart failure. The doctor warned him to avoid activities that would increase his heart rate and put additional stress on an already failing system.

He ignored it.

Camilla would patter about the mansion in her skimpiest negligee, occasionally allowing the old man to fondle her curvaceous body. He experimented with a variety of erectile dysfunction medications while fantasizing that he might be able to satisfy a woman half his age. She, on the other hand, fantasized about diving into large piles of one-hundred-dollar bills, raked into heaping mounds like leaves in the fall.

Throckmorton died shortly before their second anniversary.

Camilla put on a convincing portrayal of a grieving widow at the funeral. She practically drowned out the eulogy with her sobbing, which at times, sounded more like laughter than crying. Thankfully, the pool boy attended the service and was available to provide comfort in her time of sorrow.

Camilla insisted that Brad and Rachel be seated with the family during the service. They felt awkward and uncomfortable. The relationship between Brad and his mother had never been good. He was an unfortunate inconvenience that she was forced to drag through life. There was no mother and child bond, physical or behavioral, between them. He was too much like his father: grounded, loyal and dependable. Those were admirable qualities for servants, but not husbands or sons.

Brad and Rachel were both surprised by the amount of affection Camilla held for Cain. As far as they could tell, she had never loved anyone genuinely. What made him so special? Was she trying to make up for being such a poor mother?

Rachel didn't trust her. There had to be an ulterior motive. Cruella-Camilla never helped anyone without expecting something in return. What was the payback?

Cain would return home from his two-week sabbaticals with Grand-Mother full of questions. If someone expressed generosity, or did something nice for no apparent reason, he would twist up the corner of his mouth, scrunch his eyebrows and remark, "That's stupid. Why would anyone do that?" It usually took about a month to deprogram the thought patterns Grand-Mother embedded in his brain.

His teen years were spent dodging trouble. Always the entrepreneur, Cain was caught selling celebrity porn photos that he had printed using his home computer. His best friend's mother called Rachel to chew her out over the incident.

"If you don't get a grip on that boy, he's going to wind up in prison. He's a minor and you're accountable for his actions. They can lock you up too, you know."

They grounded him and took away all possible privileges, but none of their disciplinary actions proved effective for any length of time. Cain would wiggle in and out of one jam after another without suffering any serious consequences. He was more of an instigator than an actual participant. Unfortunate friends took the fall.

Sports didn't appeal to Cain either. He enjoyed watching others play, but all that physical contact, running, and sweating was too much like work – that nasty four letter word reserved for those who weren't smart enough to avoid it. Instead, he joined the debate team and played saxophone in the band.

Cain made excellent grades in high school despite the fact he never studied or did homework. School bored him for the most part. He did enjoy the ladies – all of them. They didn't have to be beautiful or intelligent to join his harem, just willing.

Early in his senior year, he started shopping for a college. Cain was eligible for several scholarships and his parents were more than happy to fill out a little paperwork if it would help ease the financial burden of higher education.

Camilla had other ideas.

"He's going to Harvard," she stated, matter-of-factly. "My only grandson deserves a quality education." She volunteered to cover the cost of tuition and books. In return, Cain was expected to maintain a 3.5 GPA. Mom and Dad picked up the tab for housing and living expenses.

The first semester, he called home twice a week to bring mother up to speed on the poor state of his living conditions, lack of laundry service, and how he needed more money. When she suggested he take a part-time job, the phone went silent. Rachel was beginning to wonder if she'd lost the connection, then he at last spoke.

"Let me talk to Dad."

The First National Bank of Dad was always good for a few bucks. Cain would ask to borrow money; Brad would fork it over with the unspoken agreement that it would never be repaid. Rachel would complain, but to Brad, all was well in the universe. The planets could continue their orbit around his son.

Camilla held Cain to a much higher level of accountability. Weekly phone calls and regular transcripts of his grades were required to keep the funds flowing. She also demanded to know every detail of his personal life. Who was he hanging out with? What type of social and economic background did they come from? Conversations regarding his friends always ended with her abbreviated version of a George Washington quote, "It is better to be alone than in poor company."

By the time he was a fifth-year law student, Cain had developed strong political opinions. He objected to the direction our country was headed and the for-sale-to-the-highest-bidder policies of our elected officials. He got some great publicity as an activist, making the cover of USA Today for his part in a campus anti-war rally. A little national recognition was all it took to whet his appetite for the big stage.

After graduation, he was hired to manage the campaign of an idealistic dreamer running for Congress. The man had good intentions, but was a poor public speaker and lacked the stage presence necessary to capture the imagination – or the votes – of an apathetic constituency.

Despite a lopsided pounding at the polls, Cain felt very positive about the experience. He had met a lot of shakers-and-movers, learned the ins-and-outs of fundraising, and gained valuable insight into the political process. Even more importantly, Eliana Broder had come into his life.

Eliana was built like a matchstick; a straight, shapeless body, topped with a bulbous head. Her carrot-red hair was cropped close and curved to follow the cheekbones protruding above a square jaw. Oversized glasses further magnified her doe-eyed appearance. A human Tweety Bird, ever watchful for that mean ol' Puddy Tat.

Brad and Rachel had met a lot of the girls Cain dated in high school and college. They were either very pretty, had voluptuous bodies, or both. What was so infatuating about this stick girl? Brad pulled him off to the side.

"Son, you seem to like this girl a lot. I don't mean to trash your choice in women, but . . . she's a little . . . different." Brad struggled to find the right words.

"I know, Dad. She's not gorgeous. But we have a lot in common. Our political philosophies line up, we like the same books and movies, plus – her family is loaded." He grinned and shot his Dad a little wink.

Just when his parents thought their son might be maturing to the point of looking beyond the physical attributes of a woman to search for true inner beauty, they realized it was her bank account that had him doing back-flips. Rachel wasn't surprised. "He's a chip off the ol' Cruella," she whispered to Brad.

The next weekend, he took Eliana to meet Grand-Mother. This was a first. No previous bridal candidate had made it to the Camilla inspection and approval stage. Obviously, Cain was serious about this girl.

A big fight broke out between the two women during dinner. Eliana called her a "crazy old bitch," and things just got nastier from there. Cain tried to play peacemaker, but neither side would listen. Dessert was served in flying saucers.

Camilla phoned Cain early the next morning.

"You need to marry that Jewish girl."

"What? After the knock-down-drag-out you two had last night, you want me to marry her?"

"Absolutely. That girl has spunk. She will push, pull, and drag you to become more than you could ever achieve on your own. Get down on your knees and beg if you have to. Do whatever it takes to put a ring on that girl's finger."

Cain went online to research Jewish wedding traditions. If her father offered a dowry of ten or fifteen goats, he would need a place to keep them. *Perhaps they could graze the lawn at Grand-Mother's mansion.*

Judging by their home, you'd never guess the Broders had money. It was a small house on a half-size lot in an older section of town. A couple of ten-year-old cars sat in the driveway. Inside the garage, a labyrinth of narrow trails wove through a ceiling-high assemblage of treasures collected from yard sales, thrift stores, and flea markets. If it was cheap or free, they brought it home.

Solomon Broder referred to himself an independent financial consultant. His specialty was turning some poor sap's rock pile into his gold mine. A conversation with Solomon might begin with the weather, sports, or automobiles, but it always ended with money.

"It's simple economics, my boy," he told Cain. "You buy cheap and sell high. Timing is everything."

"Father is so materialistic," complained Eliana. "He's totally consumed by his love affair with money. I get sick of hearing about it."

Solomon and Grand-Mother will get along fine, thought Cain.

The Broders adherence to Jewish traditions was similar to some Gentile attitudes toward the Ten Commandments – go with the "light" version. Pick six or seven that are agreeable, and easy to obey, and ignore the rest. Marital customs made the favored list.

Kiddushin is the Hebrew word for marriage. The groom extends a formal proposal by offering wine in the Betrothal Cup to the prospective bride. Drinking from the cup signifies her acceptance. For all intents and purposes, they are bound to each other from that moment on. All that remains is the written contract and the actual wedding ceremony itself.

After a couple of bottles of wine, legal negotiations began.

"How much for the skinny red-haired girl, Mr. Broder?"

"She would be a bargain at million dollars. Her mother and I have a lot invested in that girl."

"Yes sir, I understand. Raising a child, and putting her through college can be quite expensive. Even after graduation, daughters can continue to be a financial drain. It's always 'Daddy I need this, and Daddy I want that.'

"Tell you what I'm willing to do. I'll take this girl off your hands, provide room and board, and cover her living expenses. That will free up several thousand dollars a year in working capital you can use for other purposes. In addition, if you throw in that old Kia in the driveway, I promise you a grandchild within the next five years."

A big grin spread across Solomon's face. "You drive a hard bargain, Crofton. Make it two grandchildren and you have yourself a deal."

The wedding was held on a Saturday night at the American Legion hall near the Broder home in upstate New York. Brad and Rachel flew in on Wednesday and planned to stay at a hotel.

"Nonsense," proclaimed Solomon. "We're family now. Our house is your house."

Camilla arrived a week early to oversee arrangements for the reception. As predicted, she and Solomon were peas in a pod. Mr. Broder swore he could hear a dime drop on shag carpet at fifty yards, while Camilla fawned over the idea of developing Eau de Ben, a perfume to capture the aromatic essence of freshly printed one-hundred-dollar bills. Such conversations went on for hours – their eyes sparkling like children on Christmas morning (or in his case, Hanukah).

It's typical for mothers to cry when their children get married. Mrs. Broder and Rachel didn't fall into the stereotype. They sat there grinning like Cheshire cats while Solomon, Brad and Camilla bawled their eyes out. Rachel was just thankful there was plenty of wine at the reception.

Cain and Eliana flew to Aruba for their honeymoon. Solomon's cousin owned a travel agency and they negotiated the price down to the point where the kids were practically being paid to visit the Caribbean. Two glorious weeks laying on the beach, surfing the internet on laptops and texting each other romantic notes from eight feet away.

Back home, Brad and Rachel resumed their daily grinds. He sold auto insurance to Spanish speaking immigrants, while she taught English as a second language to underprivileged elementary kids. If her students were going to grow up to become graffiti artists, the least she could do was teach them proper spelling and punctuation.

After their honeymoon, Cain joined a law firm that specialized in personal injury cases. Eliana was a divorce attorney by day and a political activist all other waking minutes. Even their dog, Champ, was eager to help the poor, downtrodden, and defenseless – as long as there was a bone in it for him.

The only time Brad and Rachel heard from them was when they wanted something. After an eternity, they finally accepted Rachel's invitation to "friend" her on Facebook.

"Guess who's running for state senate?" Rachel asked.

"I wouldn't have a clue," replied Brad, without looking up from his morning paper.

"I think you'd recognize him. He's got his father's good looks and his grandmother's talent for charming the gullible." Rachel's response caught Brad off-guard. He spewed hot coffee out his nostrils, across the sports section, and all over his plaid boxers.

"You've got to be kidding me." Brad jumped to his feet and stumbled into their make-shift office. He leaned over her shoulder to read the monitor, a drop of coffee dangled precariously from the end of his bright red beak.

"It's posted on Facebook," said Rachel, matter-of-factly.

Brad peered at the screen. *Cain Crofton files to run for State Senate, District 13. "We are excited about this opportunity to serve our community," says Crofton." I vow to represent the voice of the people. I will fight to create jobs, abolish unfair taxes on small business and agriculture, and defend the rights of working people in District 13 and our entire state."*

"That sounds like it was copied straight from *Running for Office 101*," said Brad. "Keys for a safe and successful campaign–take the middle ground, don't offend anyone, and say what the people want to hear."

"Well, that recipe has worked for a long time. You know Cain has spent the last two years brown-nosing the governor and kissing the party chairman's ass. He wouldn't be running if it wasn't a sure thing."

"You're probably right." Brad wiped his nose on his T-shirt sleeve and headed to the kitchen for a fresh cup of coffee.

Over the next eight months, the campaign took on a life of its own. Cain ran from one place to another, shaking hands and kissing babies, while Eliana covered every ice cream social, chili cook-off, and garage sale in District 13. The governor even showed up at the county fair to endorse the Crofton camp.

"The latest poll shows Cain leading Wallace by sixteen points," said Brad. "With only six weeks to go, it looks like this thing's in the bag."

"Don't pop the champagne too soon," Rachel replied. "He may be four lengths ahead going into the last curve, but horse races are won or lost in the home stretch."

"Yeah, but Eliana is the jockey on this horse. She'll spur him to victory."

Cain proved to be a natural at mudslinging, name calling, and questioning the sanity and competence of the opposition. He kept Wallace on the defensive, pinned in a corner like a wounded mouse, to be ridiculed and abused for the enjoyment of a bloodthirsty public. Even Grand-Mother Camilla leapt from the shadows to take a few verbal slaps at Wallace in a TV ad. The Crofton campaign made politics fun for the entire family.

The state party chair proclaimed Cain a rising star after the landslide victory. One of the "old guard" took him under his wing and began mentoring the young protégé on the virtues and vices of professional politics.

"Welcome to the club, my boy," the retired senator told him. "You can have a long and lucrative career in this business by mastering one important principle – how to be bought . . . without getting caught."

By the end of his first term, Cain became fluent at speaking from both sides of his mouth. Under the tutelage of his mentor, he learned to make long-winded speeches designed to pump hope and confidence into voters without providing any real substance.

"Survival in politics means getting re-elected – repeatedly," said the senator. "Preparations for the next election should begin immediately after being sworn into office. Align your resources, refill the campaign coffers, and take the safe side on all emotional issues. Always be prepared to defend your turf. You don't want some snotty-nosed idealist to come along and knock you off the government teat."

Cain's popularity grew with each public appearance. He made himself available for every groundbreaking and ribbon-cutting photo opportunity in the manufacturing sector. School administrators invited him to speak at commencement ceremonies, and he gladly accepted all invitations to visit senior centers and children's hospitals – as long as TV cameras were there to capture the compassion.

One year into his second term as state senator, the governor called.

"Crofton, I've only got a few months left as governor due to that stupid term limit law. Somebody in our party needs to step up and file for this office. And that somebody is you."

"I don't know, Governor. I appreciate the vote of confidence, but those are pretty big shoes you're asking me to fill."

"Listen, Crofton, I inherited a helluva mess the day I was sworn in. It took six and half years to get this state back in decent shape. We can't just turn around and hand it back to those idiots. Now, call your wife and Grandma, and start figuring out what it's going to take to win the next election."

Eliana and Camilla began plotting strategy months before Cain formally announced his intention to run. Discreet phone calls, clandestine meetings, and backroom deals secured financial support from business and industry leaders.

Cain had been invited to speak at the dedication of a new veteran's memorial near the state capitol. With a large contingency of patriotic voters and statewide media coverage, it was the perfect setting to announce his candidacy.

"Today, we come together to honor those . . ." said Cain, pausing for dramatic effect, "who paid the ultimate price for our freedom. It is our duty to preserve those freedoms and defend future generations . . ." he paused again and made a sweeping gesture toward the Cub Scouts in attendance, "from all enemies, both internal, as well as those outside our borders, who seek to destroy our nation. That is why . . . I'm offering . . . myself today . . . as a candidate for governor."

"Turn the TV off," Rachel told Brad. "I've seen enough. Starting tomorrow, we'll be harassed and interrogated by every casual acquaintance and distant cousin twice-removed. I can hear them now, 'How do you think Cain will do? What kind of governor will he be?' yada-yada-yada, just like Heckle and Jeckle, talking to hear their heads rattle."

"Now, Rachel, don't be so cynical. People just like to say they know a celebrity, or at least claim to be acquainted with a friend of a friend whose ex-mother in-law once shook hands with a back stage roadie at an Elvis concert. I think it's kinda cool our son is running for governor. Just think, you can be that backstage roadie for all those folks who need a touch of celebrity to make their lives complete. You should be flattered."

Brad beamed with pride. He didn't often get a chance to say something witty and this little exchange made him feel like he was ready to join the Blue Collar Comedy tour.

Rachel rolled her eyes. "You can answer the phone calls, Mister Daddy-of-the-Governor-to-be. I'm signing up for the witness protection program."

To celebrate their fifth wedding anniversary, Eliana posted on Facebook that she was pregnant with their second child. Moments later, Grandpa Solomon clicked the "like" button, followed by Great Grandmother Camilla, who wasted no time informing the rest of the universe. In his response to Solomon, Cain commented, "This is one politician who *always* keeps his promises." Rachel nearly choked on her Cheerios when she read that line.

Eliana had filled out a little in five years. She'd traded her over-sized glasses for contacts, and finally found a hair-dresser who could do something with that red mop on top of her head. No one would mistake her for a centerfold, but at least she was starting to look like a politician's wife.

People often remark that women have a certain "glow" about them during pregnancy. When she was pregnant with Cain, Camilla referred to Rachel's as the London fog at midnight. Eliana, on the other hand, lit up like a radioactive isotope. Scientists haven't figured out if it's the attitude of the mother, or the personality of the unborn. Rachel kept her fingers crossed and hoped for the best.

The gubernatorial race required more travel than Cain's previous campaigns. Bouncing a toddler from one hotel room to another made potty training a challenge, so little Saul stayed with Brad and Rachel when his parents were on the road. He would sit on his grandmother's and clap when Mommy made a speech on TV or Daddy ridiculed an opponent in a televised debate.

Brad tried to keep an eye on Saul while Rachel fixed dinner, but the little green-eyed, red-haired gremlin was faster than chain-lightning and twice as destructive. He responded to scoldings from his grandmother with a big grin, proudly displaying the gap between his front teeth, and jabbered, "I wuv you, Memaw."

Weekends were the worst. Saul contained enough energy to power New York City. Naps were not part of his repertoire, and Grandma and Grandpa were no match for his stamina. When he did finally succumb to sleep, usually around midnight, Brad and Rachel would split a bottle of wine and collapse from exhaustion. They both agreed, raising children is a young person's job.

The governor's race proved to be a downhill jog. Cain swatted aside barbs and accusations with the ease of a bad-minton player slamming soft lobs back into his opponent's face.

"Mom, I want you and Dad to come to the capital for the watch party," said Cain.

"What about Saul? I don't think I can keep up with him in a crowd."

"You won't have to. Eliana's parents are flying down on Monday. Her mother has volunteered to watch him."

"Poor dear," Rachel murmured to herself.

"What's that, Mom?"

"Great to hear. I'm sure little Saul will keep his Grandma Broder entertained," she replied, telegraphing her smirk with bobbing eyebrows.

The purpose of a watch party is to give the candidates a chance to exhale and catch their collective breath. It's a time to relax, celebrate or console fellow party members, and hope the voters found your promises more believable than your opponent's.

Camilla swept into the hall with all the pomp and circumstance of the Queen of England. The timing of her grand entrance was orchestrated to maximize exposure and capture the attention of everyone in the room.

The media mobbed her, followed by the deep-pocketed bene-factors whom she had convinced to finance the Crofton campaign. She'd invested a fortune on her make-up, hair, and evening gown in preparation for the event. It was money well spent. The old barn looked pretty good with a new coat of paint.

Cain introduced his parents to congressmen, senators, and all the party brass. Brad hob-nobbed masterfully, exchanging meaningless pleasantries and small talk while Rachel smiled and nodded like a bobblehead.

Shortly after nine, Cain's opponent called to concede. Eliana asked the family to join them on stage for the formal media announcement. Rachel clutched Brad's arm and tried to stay hidden behind Camilla. Her second glass of wine kicked in, and she started giggling like a schoolgirl when Cain told the audience what a great governor he would be. Brad squeezed her arm and Camilla shot her the "look," while Solomon grinned at his shoes.

"What was so funny?" Brad asked her later.

"Cain's speech," she replied, still giggling. "For a minute there, I was afraid he might choke on his own humility. Wonder who he inherited that from?"

Rachel returned to work on Thursday to find a large banner draped across the blackboard behind her desk. "Congratulations, Mrs. Crofton." The students bombarded her with questions and Tanner, the mayor's son, asked if she could arrange for the governor-elect to pardon those who failed to complete their homework on election night.

The principal, teachers, and staff teased her about moving to the capitol to run the state Board of Education. "Not a bad idea," she said with a smile.

The celebrity parents role held plenty of perks. They got the best tables at restaurants, discounts on evening wear, and made the "A" list for snooty parties. For the first time since Cain entered politics, they were enjoying the attention without embarrassment.

On the down side, Rachel caught herself giving long-winded, non-committal answers to simple yes/no questions. It got so bad, one child wet her pants during the five-minute dissertation on personal hygiene while awaiting permission to use the bathroom. Rachel felt awful. *Too bad Cain wasn't here. It was a brilliant speech. He would have been so proud.*

The duties of a governor are not clearly defined, but most politicians agree it has little to do with staying home and seeing after the affairs of your state. Cain spent his first two years in office jet-setting to powwows in Washington, hanging with other governors, and volunteering for fact-finding missions in the Caribbean. Much of this was done under the pretense of attracting business and industry to his state. He did convince one company to open an office and hired a whopping thirty people to provide online technical support for poor souls who couldn't figure out how to operate a manual can opener.

Re-election came and went with only token opposition. Little Saul held a mock election in kindergarten and declared himself the winner, even though he finished third in the popular vote. Some accused him of tampering with the process and buying off the Electoral College (teacher) with lavish gifts (jewelry, perfume, etc.).

Rachel defended his actions. "That's simply not true. There's nothing wrong with a student showing his teacher a little appreciation and gratitude. After all, *teachers* mold the future of this country."

December brought cool weather and holidays. Saul and his baby sister, Jezebel, were overjoyed to celebrate both Hanukah and Christmas. Rachel watched the children opening their presents and smiled. *With a little research of Camilla's lineage, they could probably claim Kwanza as a family holiday too.*

Solomon started a bond fund in each child's name. Taking them upon his lap he extolled the virtues of collecting money as if it were butterflies or baseball cards.

"Now children, Poppa is going to teach you how to take two of these," he said, pointing to a couple of Ben Franklins on the coffee table, "and turn them into four."

"Daddy, they'll learn greed fast enough," snorted Eliana. "You should be teaching them about honor, integrity, and helping their fellow man."

"What?" Solomon's eyes shot an angry dart at his daughter. "You'd have them grow up to be paupers? There's nothing wrong with teaching these children to be self-sufficient."

Camilla slid across the room and stood by Solomon's chair, as if a battle line had been drawn across the carpet. Outnumbered and overmatched, Eliana puffed up like a blowfish and retreated to the safety of her foxhole in the kitchen.

"This younger generation," sighed Camilla, "they curse the bees while their mouths are filled with honey."

"Well said, Camilla," replied Solomon. "Very well said."

Easter Sunday brought gray skies and a mixture of sleet and rain. The grandkids had spent the night and Brad was giving them a bath prior to church and the egg hunt that would follow.

The phone rang. Rachel looked at the Caller ID – CAIN CROFTON.

"Good morning, Mom."

"Hello, son. It's nice to hear your voice. What's going on?"

"I've got some great news. Eliana and I have been talking it over . . . and I'm going to run for President."

Rachel's jaw dropped open like she'd been sucker-punched in the gut. Her stomach muscles flinched. His words knocked the breath right out of her.

"Mom? Mom, are you still there?"

She took a deep breath and responded with as much calm as she could muster.

"Why . . . would you ever want *that* job? It's nothing but a pain in the ass. You could make much more money as a senator and not have all those headaches."

"It's not about money, Mom. As President, I could do a lot to help this country."

"You've been reading too much of your own campaign literature, son. The opposition controls the House *and* the Senate. Even if you get elected, they wouldn't let you do squat."

"Well, thanks for your support! You know your problem, Mom? You see the dark side of every silver cloud. We'll be by this afternoon to pick up the kids. Good-bye."

Brad opened the bathroom door and Saul came screaming into the kitchen like a wild Indian on the warpath, followed by Jezebel, her little bathrobe stretched out in a cape.

"Who was on the phone?" asked Brad.

"It was your son," Rachel turned and looked him in the eye. "The Easter Bunny just laid a giant egg."

Brad tilted his head and cocked his eyebrows. "What are you talking about?"

"Cain is going to run for President."

"You gotta be kiddin' me. Wow! That's cool."

"Well, he'll be glad *one of us* is thrilled about it. I tried to discuss it logically with him and he got all bent out of shape – called me unsupportive."

"You've always supported him. He and Eliana are impetuous and headstrong. When they get a wild hair they act first and engage their brains later. He won't stay mad long."

Cain waited until June 6th to formally announce his candidacy. The press conference was held at the World War II Memorial in Washington, D.C. A large crowd had assembled to commemorate the Allied invasion of Europe. Cain told the audience how he planned to storm the beaches of America and break the chains of a sluggish economy, unemployment, and government oppression. He regurgitated the standard political rhetoric, and they gobbled it up like candy.

In the months leading up the caucuses and primaries, Cain became the fair-haired poster boy of the media. Comparisons to Kennedy's "Camelot" days were inevitable. He was young, handsome, energetic, and had small children. His face was plastered on the cover of *Time*, *Newsweek*, and *GQ*. *Mad* magazine's cartoon version of Eliana resembled Howdy Doody with a mullet and earrings. Rachel secretly lobbied for a Cruella DeVille bobblehead of Camilla, but to no avail.

Money poured in from across the country. Everybody wanted a piece of the action. Students established Crofton campaign headquarters on college campuses, and women voters flocked to the cause as if he were Brad Pitt modeling a clear plastic thong.

The other party contenders were no match for Cain's polished public persona. By the time the national convention rolled around, the only remaining question was who would be his running mate.

Reed Parker, a distinguished senator from Illinois, emerged as frontrunner for the job. Reed and Eliana couldn't agree on the color of grass, which was exactly the reason the party chairman and campaign manager recommended him. According to them, Parker would bring balance to the ticket and counteract Wall Street concerns regarding Cain's economic agenda. After much moaning and gnashing of teeth, the Croftons reluctantly agreed to accept Parker's offer to help save the nation. The ticket was set.

"Coffee's ready," Brad called from the kitchen.

Rachel rolled out of bed and stumbled down the hall to begin her Sunday morning ritual. Following a mandatory stop at the ladies room, she resumed her quest for the coveted easy chair in front of the TV. Brad had the coffee poured and waiting on the end table between their chairs.

The local station was running a Depends ad featuring a woman in her seventies on inline rollerskates.

"No wonder she wears Depends," said Brad. "I'd be afraid of crapping my pants too if I were on rollerblades."

"At least when the paramedics arrive she won't have an ugly brown stripe down the back of those pretty pink leotards," Rachel replied.

"Gross! What a disgusting visual image," said Brad. They laughed.

"In breaking news at this hour," the blonde-haired blue-eyed newsgirl began, "sources have confirmed the report of a two-year affair between a young woman and Presidential candidate Cain Crofton's wife, Eliana. The alleged relationship occurred while Crofton was serving in the state senate. We will have more details on this story as they become available."

Rachel wilted in her chair like a piece of cellophane in a camp-fire. Brad turned to a pillar of salt. A cigarette paper wouldn't have fit between his chin and chest. Neither of them spoke for several minutes.

"Call Cain and get the lowdown," said Rachel. "I have a feeling it's going to be a long day."

Brad dialed the number and punched speaker button. Cain answered on the first ring.

"Hi, Dad." There was a quiet sadness in his voice. "Did you and Mom watch the news this morning?"

"Yes, we did. How is Eliana holding up?"

"Not too good. She's been crying nonstop . . . says it's going to cost us the election, and worrying about Saul getting teased at school. Parker is really pissed. He threatened to pull out and hung up on me before I could get a word in edgewise. Our campaign manager scheduled a meeting this morning to discuss strategy. We will issue a statement sometime today, but right now, I don't know how we are going to respond."

"Were you aware of this affair?" asked Brad.

"Oh yeah, Eliana and I don't keep secrets. And, it could get a lot worse too if that nanny we had at the governor's mansion decides to open her damn mouth. Do you have any advice on how I should handle this?"

"Well," said Brad, in his most fatherly Ward Cleaver tone, "be as open and honest as you can without providing any details. The American people respect honesty. You're not the first politician to be caught in a sex scandal and I doubt you'll be the last. Keep your chin up. Your Mother and I will always be here for you."

"Thanks, Dad. That means a lot."

Monday morning came way too soon. The mirror revealed a fully-stuffed duffle bag under each of Rachel's eyes. She hadn't slept thirty minutes all night, and her reflection in the mirror shot back images of a wasted zombie posing for a mug shot. The two bites of stale donut she choked down for breakfast bobbed helplessly on a sea of churning stomach acid. Three cups of coffee further aggravated the storm.

She had not dreaded going to school this much since picture day in eighth grade when her mother forced her to wear a hideous floral print dress with a Pilgrim-style collar. To add further humiliation, her mom curled, teased, and tortured her hair until it rose in a peculiar nest-like fashion. Birds, squirrels, and a roving band of blind mice cast lots to see who would take up permanent residency in the penthouse above her ears. Old friends still pulled out that yearbook and cackled about the photo.

Today would be even worse.

Rachel's classroom was the third on the left from the west-wing door. she harbored fantasies of slipping in unnoticed, zipping through the day, and escaping in a rush of students when the final bell rang.

It was not be.

Sandra, Debi, and Wanda – her fellow teachers – were huddled up drinking coffee just beyond her door. One of them saw her out of the corner of her eye, whispered something to the others, and they scattered like cockroaches under a floodlight.

A few minutes before class one of the students, Cody Davis, approached Rachel's desk with a Ziploc bag full of brownies.

"These are for you. My mom said you might not be feeling too good today."

Her pent up emotions came rushing forth like lava from a volcano. In twenty-two years of teaching she had never let her students see her cry. She sobbed uncontrollably for what seemed like an eternity – probably two or three minutes. The children encircled her and encased their teacher a giant group hug. Their outpouring of genuine compassion only made her cry harder. It was a sweet relief.

By lunch time, she had regained composure and worked up enough nerve to visit the teachers' lounge. From beyond the door, she could hear people laughing and having a good time, but the second she walked in a straight pin could've been heard if it bounced on shag carpet. Most of the teachers offered nervous goodbyes and retreated to their classrooms. Only Mike and Sam remained. Sam offered half-hearted condolences regarding Cain's "little problem," as he put it, while Mike nodded his head in sad agreement.

"Thanks," was all she could mumble as they headed for the door.

The next morning Rachel was summoned to the principal's office. Eleanor White sat behind her desk and Phillip Jackson, superintendent of schools, occupied the plush wing-back leather chair to her right.

"Rachel, we have a problem." Eleanor was never one to mince words. "We've had several parents call expressing their concern over the incident regarding Cain's wife. Phillip and I believe it may be best for all parties for you to take a leave of absence until the election is over."

"What?" Rachel couldn't believe it. "I'm being expelled from school because my daughter in-law had a lesbian affair? Do they think it's some kind of contagious disease that can be spread by incidental contact?"

"No, no, nothing like that," said Phillip. "It's just that having the mother of a presidential candidate teaching at our school has created somewhat of a distraction. This additional publicity could negatively impact the children's ability to process and retain the curriculum."

"I don't think you have to worry about the children." Rachel's face flushed with anger. "The parents are the ones who are distracted by the negative publicity."

"Nevertheless," said Eleanor, "the decision has been made. You are not to return to this school until after Christmas break.

The political paparazzi tracked down every female Eliana had ever had contact with, from kindergarten to her hair stylist to the check-out girl at the grocery store. Reports of Eliana smiling at, waving to, and (gasp!) touching the naked arm of innocent women came pouring in. When a major porn magazine offered a million dollar bounty, the aforementioned nanny traded her self-respect for a life-long legacy as a used sex toy.

In an exclusive three-page interview, she supplied stroke-by-stroke details of her *ménage a trois* with the Croftons. Her pictorial, entitled *Affairs of the State*, featured the poor, abused nanny in a variety of unusual poses that only a contortionist could perform.

"It's amazing," Rachel remarked, "how flexible former government employees can be when given the proper incentive. Too bad don't see that kind of effort from those who are fully dressed."

The late-night talk show hosts and stand-up comedians were in seventh heaven. *Saturday Night Live* did a series of skits where the actors portraying Cain and Eliana seduced world leaders. Apparently, a Crofton-style foreign relations policy would be highly effective in soothing tension at "hot spots" around the globe.

Parker, who had reluctantly agreed to stay on the ticket, was not immune to scrutiny either. Investigations revealed no history of sexual indiscretion (even his hand denied that they'd ever had relations), only a lust for money. Allegations of insider trading popped up like dandelions after a spring shower. Reed claimed he only served as a consultant and never profited directly from any of those activities. Neither the media nor an apathetic public believed a word of it. The story was so dry and boring it blew away in the first little puff of breeze. Who cares about illegal stock trades when there's a juicy sex scandal waiting to be devoured?

Cain's ratings in the polls fell like an anvil from an airplane. Major sponsors pulled their support and prominent party leaders enrolled in a witness protection program rather than endorse his campaign. The rats were fleeing the ship.

Cain stalled and procrastinated as long as he could. Rumors and innuendoes dominated the headlines. Political analysts proclaimed his defeat and began spewing epitaphs of Crofton self-destruction.

It was time for Cain to grab the stick, yank back with both hands, and pull out of the nosedive, or go down in flames. In a primetime news conference, he pled his case to the American people.

"If you've been anywhere near planet Earth in the last thirty days, you are aware of the gossip and allegations regarding sexual improprieties reportedly committed by my wife and myself. Without going into detail, I will tell you that some are true, some are false, and all have been wildly exaggerated. Like most people, Eliana and I have done things in the past that we regret with great embarrassment." Cain paused, swallowed hard, and put on his best 'whipped puppy' expression. "I say this not to condone or justify such behavior, but as a simple confession of imperfect humanity.

"These events are in the past. We cannot change them or make them go away through wishful thinking or denial. All we can do is learn from the past and strive to move forward with a strong resolve to walk uprightly before God and man."

He paused again, face strained, like a cat about to puke a giant hairball of genuine sincerity.

"I assure you that we are filled with remorse. I apologize for the pain these incidents have caused our family, our party, and those who have supported us through the years. And I humbly implore your forgiveness.

"Now, as we move forward, let us close *this* chapter and redirect our focus to the issues facing our nation." Cain wet his lips and tossed a sly smile to the young reporter in the front row who repeatedly crossed her shapely legs beneath a short skirt.

"The wolves of poverty and unemployment claw at the door of many American homes. Our businesses and corporations struggle to compete in a global economy. And we have fallen behind in education, technology, and innovation.

"The world has long looked to the United States for leadership. In recent years we have failed to meet this challenge. This November, we have an opportunity to reverse those trends and reclaim our position as a world leader."

Cain lowered his eyebrows and locked a steely gaze directly into the camera.

"Do not allow your vision to be clouded by those who would use the indiscretions of my past as a smoke-screen to distract you from the broken promises and ineffective leadership of the current administration. We cannot afford to tread water for four more years, while the rest of the world passes us by. Let us work together and restore America to her former greatness – for the sake of our children – and all future generations."

Political pundits, Wall Street analysts, and part-time bartenders sliced, diced, and made julienne fries from Cain's speech. His opponents dismissed it as hogwash, and his supporters (what few he had left) proclaimed it a modern Gettysburg Address.

The only opinion that really mattered belonged to John Q. Public.

Cain expected to see an immediate reaction in the polls. A positive bounce would show Wall Street that he could still manipulate public opinion with charm and charisma. It didn't happen.

A great Ice Age crept over Cain's numbers. For two weeks they lay frozen at an all-time low. The twenty-one percent of Americans he'd held before the speech were still there. Most of that crowd knew little or nothing about politics. They just admired the Croftons' sexually adventurous lifestyle.

The only voter block that showed any growth was the Uncommitted. From the sound of their name you'd think this group had barely passed a sanity test and were fortunate to be living outside an asylum, but for decades these wishy-washy, fence straddling, let's-see-which-way-the-wind-blows Americans have had the final say as to who sits in the White House.

Cain's opponent was a two-term Congressman from Nevada named Ansel Drucker. A short, pudgy man with the personality of a turnip, Drucker's claim to fame was the mismanagement of a chain of Las Vegas casinos, although how anyone can turn a loss in that business is one of the great mysteries of all time. Hollywood exercise guru, Leanne Tone, speculated that Ansel (which she pronounced Hansel) spent too much time at the buffet, thus consuming profits the old fashioned way – he ate them.

Drucker's idea of hitting the campaign trail meant stopping at every pizza joint, burger chain, and fried chicken stand in America. News clips showed him clutching a drumstick while planting greasy kisses on the cheeks of small children. He did more to promote childhood obesity in six months than Ronald McDonald had accomplished in forty years.

As the presidential race entered the home stretch, dates were scheduled for the final two debates– the first in early October, and the second two weeks before Election Day. Drucker's campaign manager expressed concern.

"Sir, I believe you should reconsider debating Crofton," he said. "You're ahead by twenty-five points. There's nothing to gain by going head-to-head with him on national TV."

"I know, I know," said Drucker, "but the American people want it. They expect it. If I refuse to debate Crofton they'll accuse me of being scared. I want to show them I'm a strong leader, not afraid to face tough challenges. We've been kicking Crofton's ass for months. It's time to stomp the little pervert like a grape – then move into the White House."

The October debate could be summarized as two overgrown school boys pointing fingers and yelling at each other. Each spent a great deal of time tattling on his opponent while painting himself as a brave knight in shining armor, ready to risk life and limb to save the nation. The dragons of unemployment, national debt, health care, and education slept through the entire performance – only raising their heads for an occasional yawn.

The American people weren't impressed either. In fact, few even bothered to watch. Football season was in full swing and the holidays were just around the corner. Moving the large hump of the bell-shaped curve – the undecided voters – would require more than same old tired political rhetoric.

Drucker maintained a large lead heading into the final debate. He didn't have to win – just hold onto the ball and run out the clock. Cain, on the other hand, needed a last-second miracle.

It was time to unleash the beast.

Marty Schall had been hired as campaign manager for one reason – results. Ruthless and despicable were his second and third middle names. If the man held a single redeeming character trait, he kept it locked in a dungeon for recreational purposes. His beady eyes, elongated ski-jump nose, and greasy black hair further promoted a rat-like appearance. He spoke out of the left corner of his mouth, upper lip hiked like a dog's hind leg, spewing curse words from behind yellow teeth.

Schall summoned Cain, Parker and the entire campaign staff to a Marriott conference room outside Baltimore. The mood inside was as gray and dismal as the cold drizzle that ran like frightened teardrops down the windows facing Fort McHenry.

It made people's skin crawl just to be in the same room with him. After the election, it was learned he was a direct descendant of Herta Bothe, a top-five female Nazi war criminal known for her sadistic brutality. Eliana became physically sick upon hearing the news, and poor Solomon flirted with cardiac arrest – both had shaken his hand.

"Crofton," snapped Schall, "how long are you going to let that fat bastard kick your ass? Is your Grandma the only one in this family with any balls?"

Cain rose from his chair, eyebrows scrunched and face flushed with anger.

"You little shit. I ought to kick your ass."

"I don't think so, Mr. I-Run-a-Clean-Campaign. You're too damn nice. Drucker keeps tossing you soft lobs, but instead of knocking 'em out of the park . . . you want to bunt. Wake up, Crofton. It's the bottom of the ninth, two out, and you're trailing by three runs. You gotta hit a grand slam if you want to win the freakin' game."

"And how am I going to do that?" asked Cain, sarcastically.

"Well, first you gotta get some runners on base. It's easy. Find some illegal activities here, some ethics violations there. Chip away at his character. Plant some doubt and distrust in the voters' mind. And when he starts back-pedaling . . . POW! A swift kick in the nuts.

"It's time to get personal, Crofton. There are skeletons in every closet. You just have to dig around a little to find them. Lard Boy probably keeps his hid behind a mountain of Girl Scout cookies.

"Hmmm . . ." Schall's expression changed. He stared blindly into space and chewed his lower lip. The wheels between his ears spun like a meth-crazed hamster on an exercise wheel.

"Hey, I just remembered something I need to check on. I'll catch up with you guys later."

"Do you think he forgot to unplug the iron?" Cain grinned at Eliana.

"I doubt it," she replied. "He doesn't know what one is."

"Jeremy, see if you can get this damn computer to work" Drucker licked the donut glaze from his fingers and handed the laptop to a young staff worker. "It runs like a tortoise, and when you try to open a file, it locks up. What a piece of junk."

"Sounds like a virus, sir." Jeremy's nimble fingers whacked away at the keys and tapped on the sticky mouse pad, but to no avail.

"If you can't figure it out, find somebody who knows how to fix it." Drucker exhaled in disgust. "I've got some files in there that haven't been backed-up, all my emails, and a recipe for the best hot wings you ever wrapped your lips around."

"No problem, sir. There's a computer repair store a couple of blocks from here. I'll have them make it a top priority."

"Tell 'em it's a matter of national importance. Our country's future rests in their hands." Drucker grinned. "And see if they'll donate the labor."

It was three days until the final debate. The constant travel and daily boot-licking of every splinter group along the trail created a physical and emotional drain — especially on a fat man pushing seventy. Drucker was as anxious for the election to be over as the millions of Americans who were tired of being pounded day and night with political ads. If it hadn't been for all the buffets and $1,000-a-plate fund raisers along the way, he would have dropped out half-way through the primaries.

Now, with two weeks to go, the comfortable lead he maintained over Crofton gave him confidence he would soon supplant William Howard Taft as the fattest President in American history. A couple of celebrity chefs were already busy planning a menu for the inaugural dinner. He began to salivate just thinking about it.

The department's IT specialists were still combing the hard drive when Detective Lowry arrived. He'd worked a few of these cases before, but never with such a high-profile perp. The implications were monumental. Every detail of the investigation would be questioned, challenged, and dissected by the best lawyers money could buy. There was no margin for error.

"What-da-ya-got, kid?" Lowry peered over the shoulder of a young man scanning files on a laptop.

"Pornographic images of young girls. What's really weird is the way they're dressed – if you want to call it that."

"What do you mean?"

"Here, look at this."

A photo of a pre-teen girl popped on the screen. She was nude except for a Girl Scout beret and a pair of hiking boots. A couple of Thin Mint cookies, strategically placed, served as pasties. The theme continued throughout the folder. Shortbread, Peanut Butter Sandwich, Caramel deLights, all found their way into compromising positions.

Lowry closed his eyes and turned away.

"Where's the guy that found these files? We need to talk."

"He's in the parts room. Anderson is getting a statement from him now."

Colin Brewer, the owner and sole technician of *Click to Fix*, sat perched upon a stool behind a small workbench. The closet-sized parts room was an absolute hoarder's heaven. Pizza boxes, PC boards, candy wrappers, and magazines left little room for human intrusion. Anderson stepped out to make room for the detective.

"Can you verify those files were on the laptop when it came in?" asked Lowry.

"Yes, sir. I was scanning the hard drive for malware and came across a folder named GS. When I opened it and saw the kiddie porn, I called the police."

"Do you know who the owner is?"

"The guy that dropped it off said it belonged to Ansel Drucker. He wanted me to stop what I was doing and give this top priority. Offered me an extra hundred bucks if I could have it done by 5 pm."

"Do you know who Ansel Drucker is?"

"Yes, sir. He's the short, fat guy who's running for president."

"Then you understand the importance of keeping your mouth shut until we complete our investigation. Right now, the only people who know those files exist are you, us, and the person who downloaded them. If anything pops up on Facebook, Twitter, or other media, I'll be back to arrest you for impeding an investigation. Got it?"

Brewer lowered his eyes, bit his lip, and nodded.

Cain and Eliana were going over a list of perspective questions for the final debate. She grilled him like a piece of raw meat, stopping just short of throwing him to the dogs. It didn't do much for the relationship, but his answers were honed to a razor-sharp edge.

She could see Cain was reaching the breaking point. Time to ease the tension.

"Governor Crofton, what's your position on group sex now that your wife has admitted her taste for women?"

Cain made eye contact. She could see the smile start to grow. It burst into a huge grin, followed by laughter, then coughing, and finally, tears rolling down his rounded cheeks.

"Well, so far," he could barely talk for laughing, "I haven't found a single position I didn't like."

Eliana smiled. Mission accomplished.

Her cell phone buzzed. Text message from Camilla Throckmorton. *Drucker caught with child porn. Turn on your TV.*

They searched frantically for the remote. Cushions flew, papers scattered, fifteen minutes later the CNN anchor confirmed the news.

"Did he say Girl Scouts?" asked Cain. "I could see him fantasizing about the cookies, but not kids. This is too good to be true."

Lowry leaned back in his chair and stewed. That little nerd, Brewer, had let the cat out of the bag before the police arrived. One quick tweet and the whole world knew about it in a manner of minutes.

Drucker and his lawyers were on their way downtown for questioning. He didn't expect to get much out of them except denials and accusations of sabotage. Then they'd blame him for the leak and the media circus that would follow.

Everything followed script from that point. Both lawyers talked at once and Drucker, who had clearly been crying, sat hollow-eyed, staring into space. They produced a list of names, people who had possible access to the laptop. This would be a fast and furious investigation. They demanded Senator Drucker be cleared immediately.

Lowry pulled open his desk drawer and reached for the Advil.

Viewers tuned in to watch the final debate in record numbers. If the producers had thrown in a few "Super Bowl quality" commercials it would have likely unseated the final episode of *M*A*S*H* as the most watched program in television history.

Human beings are endowed with a certain morbid curiosity. Three days of non-stop media pounding had left Drucker wounded and bleeding. Part of the audience hoped their hero would rise from the mat, overcome all odds, and deliver a miraculous knock-out blow like Rocky Balboa. The majority wanted to see Cain go for the jugular and finish Drucker off in gladiator fashion.

There was nothing new or earth-shattering about the questions themselves.

"Governor Crofton," began the moderator, "how do you plan to address our trade deficit with China?"

"The United States economy, and that of China, are both dependent upon the relationship of our two countries." Cain smiled at the camera and rambled through the allotted response time extolling the virtues of free trade in a global economy, never actually answering the question.

"Senator Drucker," said the moderator. "Do you believe America should take military action in the Middle East to quell the threat of nuclear weapons?"

"Well, I . . . ah, my administration . . . we plan to . . . ." Drucker stumbled through his words like a school boy who'd peed his pants during an oral book report. He was shaken, nervous, and unprepared.

Those who tuned in expecting to see a heavy-weight match-up witnessed a lopsided pummeling. Drucker was on the ropes from the opening bell. His answers were weak punches, flailing harmlessly through thin air. Cain responded with powerful blows and sharp jabs.

Prior to the debate, both parties agreed to disallow sex scandal questions. It didn't matter. The elephant in the room circled both participants before camping out beside Drucker, wrapping his invisible trunk around the torso, and winking at the camera.

Political analysts regurgitated key points and profound rhetoric, as if issues really mattered. In ten days the American people would have their say.

"How's the investigation going?"

Lowry was so sick of that question he could puke. It didn't help that Drucker's lawyers called every fifteen minutes, or that they'd hired a dozen private investigators to constantly second-guess his every move.

Paparazzi circled like vultures. Their telescopic cameras recorded every feeble excuse for movement by the dog-pile of detectives working the case.

The muckrakers weren't interested in facts. Facts don't sell tabloids. All they wanted was a photo to decorate the dirt some highly imaginative fiction writer had generated to spawn a feeding frenzy in the magazine aisle at Walmart.

Lowry rapped on the Captain's door, then let himself in without waiting for a response.

"Chief, I want off the case."

"No." The Captain never looked up.

"And why not?"

"You're the worst bullshitter in the department. Drucker knows it, his lawyers, the press, everybody. Lowry, you couldn't candy-coat a piece of fudge and make it palatable. You'd refuse to be politically correct if the other option was castration."

"That's right. And that'll happen too if I stay on the case."

"No it won't, and I'll tell you why. The investigation has been going on for six days and we cannot prove those files were loaded by Senator Drucker – or ever viewed by him. Too many people had access to the laptop. There's not enough evidence to convict him beyond a reasonable doubt. We don't have a case."

"Good. Now, we can all go back to our hot chocolate and tiddlywinks and pretend it never happened."

"Humph." The thin smile forced its way onto the captain's face. "We will. Just as soon as you attend the press conference Drucker's lawyers scheduled this afternoon and tell the world that while the investigation is still ongoing, we have no evidence to link Senator Drucker to the files."

"They were on *his* laptop." Hair began to rise on the back of Lowry's neck. "If it were anybody else, *that* would be enough."

"Well, *he* is who he is – and it *isn't* enough." The captain leaned forward and glared at Lowry. "Now, get your ass down there and look pretty on TV."

"But why me? Why not send 'Mr. Sunshine' down there to do your talking?"

"Because you have something he doesn't."

"And what's that?"

"Credibility."

The press conference began with a brief, prepared statement, read by Lowry.

Reporters shouted questions as he left the podium. He responded with a monotone, cookie-cutter reply. "No further comment. This is an ongoing investigation."

Drucker's Chief of Staff took center stage and declared the Senator absolved of any wrongdoing. He spent the next twenty minutes sprinkling innuendoes and tossing barbed insults at the Crofton camp, stopping just short of a public accusation of cyber espionage.

Rachel reached for the remote and switched the channel. "Can you believe they're letting him off?"

"Yes. Yes, I can," said Brad. "This is politics, honey. Too many people have too much money riding on this thing to let it go down without a fight. You've been around enough to know that."

"I know, but this just seems so . . . *nasty*." Rachel drew back her hands, fingers drooping like they were covered in poop, shaking them vigorously between fake gags.

Brad grinned. "You do that well. I bet Schall could arrange to have you guest host *Saturday Night Live*."

"Don't even think about it, Mister. Besides, the public wouldn't like me."

"They might not all love you as much as I do. But it would certainly make for an entertaining evening."

Drucker's campaign ads pounded the American public like softball-sized hail on a aluminum pie-plate. There was nowhere to run. No concrete bunker thick enough, no redneck numbskull dense enough to withstand the constant bombardment.

As Election Day neared, people were beginning to buy in. The conspiracy theory sold well to those who didn't want to believe a sweet old man with an eating disorder would collect pictures of naked Girl Scouts.

He made it an easy pill to swallow.

"With God as my witness," declared a tearful Drucker, "I am not a pedophile. I do not like little girls in that way."

Cain and Eliana spent the final weekend darting from one battleground state to another to ensure that all important party bosses had their boots properly licked before herding their sheep to the shearing house.

"How was your two-hour stop in Florida?" asked Eliana. "Is Volker coming through like he promised?"

"He assures me it's in the bag," said Cain. "Are your Jewish friends in New York gonna help us bring home the bacon?"

"It's kosher. As long as they get the pork barrel projects you promised."

"Well, I'd hate to keep a Jew from his pork," said Cain. "Remind me to invite 'em to the White House for ribs sometime."

"I'll do that." Eliana laughed. "I'll even get you a kippah to wear for the occasion."

Two hours after the polls closed on the west coast, it was too close to call. Commentators flip-flopped like a large rodents forecasting the weather on February 2nd. Some said Cain saw his shadow, some said he didn't. As for Drucker, there was no doubt about his shadow. The only argument was how much of America it would blanket.

Four battleground states drew most of the attention. Rachel, Brad, and Solomon huddled around a small television while Camilla Velcroed herself to a recently divorced CEO of a Fortune 500 company.

"Governor Crofton," a reporter asked, "with sixty-percent of precincts reporting in Colorado, you have a one-and-a-half point lead. Are you feeling confident about your chances there?"

"It's better than being two points behind," Cain said with a grin. "We feel pretty good about our chances."

This line of questioning repeated itself every three minutes. Cain ran through the gamut with all major networks like a runaway squirrel in a hamster cage.

By two a.m., most of the guests at Drucker's 'Victory Feast' had waddled to the nearest couch for a power nap. The Jolly Fat Man proclaimed optimism.

"We're gonna win this thing. I got confidence in the American people – and when they have spoken, we will be victorious."

When the sun came over the Potomac Wednesday morning, ninety-eight percent of the vote was in. Cain led by four electoral points and only trailed by a few thousand in the popular vote.

Drucker called to concede.

"Well, Crofton, you kicked my ass. It was a hard-fought battle, but I'm a big enough man to know when I'm licked. Congratulations, Governor. Do us proud."

"Thank you, Ansel. I'm honored to serve our country."

Inauguration Day brought heavy snow. Only Saul and Jezebel seemed to appreciate the nasty weather. The newly elected "first kids" darted from their mother's side and scooped up enough snow to pelt the Secret Service men trying to corral them.

Everyone else turned their collars to the wind and prayed the inaugural speech wouldn't go into extra innings.

Cain repeated the oath of office in record time. The crowd applauded loud and long, warming their chilled bones behind a thin veil of enthusiasm. Cain drank in the frozen smiles and roaring cheers and addressed his shivering audience.

"Today," he began, pausing for dramatic effect. "We stand on the doorstep of a new America. An America of opportunity for *ALL* people" The spectators roared. "This will not be an easy journey. There will be struggles and difficulties along the way. But by working together we can forge a new future. One of security and prosperity for this generation, and those yet to come."

The crowd jumped up and down, cheering like toddlers on a sugar high. The cotton candy effect of Cain's words began to wear off after the first twenty minutes. Forty-five minutes later, he mercifully wrestled the last sentence into submission.

As the President and First Family left the stage the band attempted to play "Hail to the Chief." Lips and fingers frozen into position, the music was more reminiscent of a group of alley cats moaning a midnight mating call than an actual song.

Eliana snuggled next to Cain in the Presidential limousine, laying her head on his shoulder.

"You're one long-wind SOB, President Crofton," she sighed.

The inaugural dinner was scheduled to begin in one hour and Rachel was still trying to get feeling back in her feet.

"Do you think it'd be all right if I wore my boots?"

"I doubt the President would mind." Brad flashed a little smirk. "But his grandmother might say something."

"I could care less what *she* thinks. This night is not about her, though I'm sure she'll do whatever it takes to get her share of attention."

"Good. Then no one will be looking at us. We can blend into the background, smile and nod like bobbleheads. In a few hours it'll all be over."

"The party may end, but our lives will never be the same." Rachel turned and looked Brad square in the eyes.

"We're not in Kansas anymore, Toto."

The Land of OZ analogy proved prophetic. The room was full of talking heads, a few tin men, and one old cowardly lion. The wicked witch, Camilla, had him pinned in a corner, grilling him to tears with small talk.

"What do you think of the table settings?" she asked. "Eliana would have gone with the Kmart Blue-light Specials if I hadn't stepped in. This French provincial pattern is much more elegant and fitting for the occasion, don't you think? I swear, that girl would serve guests with paper plates and plastic sporks if you'd let her."

"Uh, yes ma'am. They are very pretty," he stammered. "Well, I'd better be . . . "

"The centerpieces were flown in from South America. A friend of mine owns the largest floral plantation in Bolivia. He donated them as a gift in my honor."

"Oh – there's my wife. It's been nice visiting with you, Mrs. Throckmorton." The old lion tucked his tail and darted for freedom.

An announcer walked to the podium and tapped the microphone. "Ladies and gentlemen, the President and First Lady of the United States of America."

Cain and Eliana strode into the room. Cain bowed and began shaking hands with congressmen and foreign dignitaries. Eliana wore a red sequin gown and ruby slippers, which she was careful not to click together. This Dorothy had no intention of returning to Kansas or any other state in Mid-America until the next campaign.

After the meal, Solomon rose, chimed an empty glass with a dinner knife, and offered a toast.

"On behalf of Camilla, Rachel, Brad, Mrs. Broder, and myself, we offer our loving support to this presidency and its administration. May they find success in all their endeavors, unify this great country, and create an environment where all nations can co-exist in peace."

When the applause died, Rachel leaned over and whispered to Brad.

"I bet he's been working on that speech for weeks."

"Longer," said Brad. "He wrote the first draft election night and has been polishing it ever since. Eliana told Cain the original version mentioned Israel three times."

After more toast and presentations by kings, princes, and potentates, the orchestra opened with a waltz. Cain led Eliana to the center of the room and swept her gracefully across the floor like Prince Charming and Cinderella on a wind-up music box.

The wait-staff scampered about like munchkins, refilling glasses of champagne and wine. Rachel began to loosen up after the third glass. She danced with Brad, Cain, and even Camilla's escort. Each time she returned, her glass had been topped off.

"I'm not a half-empty kind of girl." She smiled and toasted Brad. "I'm three-quarters full – especially tonight."

"Maybe I should get you back to our room." Brad grinned. "I might want to take advantage of the situation."

A reporter stopped them on the way out the door.

"Mrs. Crofton, do you have anything to say as your son begins his presidency?"

Rachel paused, pursed her lips, and took on a serious tone.

"May God have mercy . . . uh, I mean, may God *bless* the United States of America."

The Food Triangle

Proper nutrition is more important than ever in today's fast-paced, high-tech world. It takes a lot of energy to keep up with the demands of ungrateful teenagers, a self-absorbed husband, and a less-than-sympathetic employer.

In Grandma's day, stay-at-home moms fretted over the five basic food groups while darning socks or sewing a new apron for Aunt Jill's birthday. The family gathered around the dining table for the evening meal where Dad, Junior, and Sissy would share exciting news of the day's accomplishments while Mom stared wistfully into space, wishing she actually had a life.

No one seemed to care, or appreciate, that she'd sacrificed the best part of her afternoon (the half-hour between *The Edge of Night* and *Queen for a Day*), contemplating which fruits, veggies, and dairy products to incorporate into the family diet. They were too busy with their incessant babbling to notice the carefully measured portions and precise balance of carbohydrates to protein.

Working women in the twenty-first century don't have the time or patience to pattern meals in accordance with an old-fashioned food pyramid. Pharaoh and the kids are lucky if they get a granola bar on the way out the door. After that, they're on their own.

Between working late, soccer practice, and cheerleader tryouts, no one gathers round the dining table anymore.

Burgers and pizza may be fine for the rest of the family, but they fail miserably at providing the necessary energy and stamina for a hardworking career mother who doubles as a shuttle driver and family scheduling coordinator.

That's why I invented the food triangle.

This simple, easy-to-follow, program is built upon the Three C's – Caffeine, Chocolate, and Cocktails. Here's how it works.

For breakfast, jumpstart your morning with large Mocha Espresso. For best results, I recommend a double-shot of espresso, four squares of chocolate, and two inches of whipped cream on top. This healthy meal provides all the vitamins and minerals necessary to keep you hopping around the office like a gray squirrel on meth. You'll be amazed at how much you get done and that you were able to stay awake during that oh-so-boring presentation the VP of Finance gave on saving toilet tissue – the so called, 'Charmin Sustainability Project.'

If you start to feel a mid-morning energy lag, as many of us do, reach for a Jolt. Jolt comes in three flavors; Cola, Red Eye, and my favorite, Electric Blue. If not available in your area, chug a couple of Mountain Dews with a few chocolate donuts from the vending machine. When lunch time comes, you won't be hungry and your co-workers will be envious of your self-discipline and willpower in staying with that new diet.

By mid-afternoon it's back to the vending machine. Treat yourself to a Hershey bar and find a pot where the coffee has been cooked down to the consistency of mud. Break the candy into chunks and dissolve in the "Black Gold." Stir vigorously. Be sure to use a metal spoon and ceramic mug for this step. Otherwise, the cleaning people will be all over you when the mixture eats through the Styrofoam and chews through all seven layers of floor polish.

By five o'clock, the edge is starting to wear off and you need a little pick-me-up. A large sweet tea with extra sugar will help you navigate through the maze of idiots on the highway. I like the real syrupy kind that's sticky enough to form a permanent bond when you need to repair a dangling fingernail or reattach the heel of your shoe.

After three hours of zig-zagging a van full of demanding, smartass teenagers from one unknown location to another, Happy Hour finally arrives.

Cocktails are the most important and, by far, the most nutritious block of the food triangle. Bourbon is derived from corn, vodka from potatoes, and if you're feeling particularly frisky, add a stalk of celery to your Bloody Mary.

If you have a taste for fruit, add a splash of cranberry, orange, or grapefruit juice to gin or spiced rum to ensure that you're getting 100% of your daily requirement of vitamin C. Sometimes it takes two or three servings to get up to 100%. Don't feel guilty. Staying healthy requires determination and sacrifice. You're doing what's best for your body.

Old-school nutritionists may proclaim, "Everything in moderation." But who are you going to listen to? Those who sit around munching dried figs and baled wheat, or someone who lives in the real world?

It's your body. If you don't take care of it, who will?

Dodging Miss Daisy

On the way to work this morning, I came up behind a PT Cruiser with a bright yellow sign on the rear. "NEW DRIVER," it screamed, in big, bold, capital letters.

It's always important to know what kind of idiot you're sharing the road with, so I slid over into the left lane and crept forward to get a better look at this "new" person.

The driver turned out to be a forty-something woman, with a cigarette dangling from her lower lip. That didn't exactly fit my criteria of "new." There was no sparkle to her aura; in fact there was no aura at all. The only glow emanating from the vehicle was the cherry on her Marlboro Light. I assumed this woman's purpose in life was to teach teenagers to drive. One advantage of sending your kid to a chain-smoking driving instructor is that they'll learn how to survive in an oxygen-deprived environment. This may come in handy if they go on to become a bartender or choose to live in a submarine.

My morning commute is typically filled with sleepy-eyed Johns, munching on sausage biscuits while juggling a steaming cup of Joe. I like to get about a car length in front of them and slam on my brakes at irregular intervals. There's nothing like giving Willie Winky a hot bath on a cold morning to get the ol' blood pumping.

Some men follow me for blocks, or attempt to pull up beside my car to offer their gratitude. I appreciate the friendly hand gestures and loud words of encouragement, but I'm much too humble to take credit for teaching them the value of cup holders, so I just turn up the stereo and pretend no one else is around.

Working women face an even more daunting challenge. After sleeping till the last possible second, they leap from bed, send hubby off to work, and get the kids ready for school or daycare. This leaves no time for the all-important chore of "putting on one's face."

That's why I encouraged my teenage daughter to sign up for the Maybelline Advanced Drivers Course for women. (Pardon me while I rave about how wonderful and patient the instructors are in this class.) Normally, this is an eight-week course, but my Regina knocked it out in only four.

They start with basic left knee steering, then add more complicated maneuvers as the student becomes comfortable and gains confidence in hands-free operation of the vehicle. To graduate, attendees must be able to safely navigate the freeway at seventy-miles-per-hour, simultaneously text their best friend with one hand, apply mascara with the other, and scream at unruly children in the back seat. Upon completion, the girls receive a Beauty of the Boulevard ankle bracelet and a gift certificate for Maybelline eye-care products.

I couldn't be prouder of that girl, but there's no way I'm getting in a car with *her* behind the wheel.

New drivers, like Regina, tend to be road-hazards due to over-confidence. At that age, they're swinging the world by the tail and feel twelve-foot-tall and bullet-proof. Nothing bad has ever happened to them, so why should they worry about it now?

I loved the look on Regina's face when I handed her that first auto insurance bill. Miss Priss sure tumbled from her pedestal that day. Welcome to my world, Sister.

The only thing more dangerous than new drivers is old drivers. God, they scare the crap out of me.

It doesn't bother me that they're old, or that they suffer from a massive dose of incompetence, diarrhea, constipation, and gout. Heck, I can even live with their poor vision, slow reaction time, failure to use turn signals, and the inability to accelerate beyond forty miles-per-hour. What gets me is the times of day they choose to invade our highways.

For some reason, every appointment they make has to be first thing in the morning. Whether it be the doctor, hairdresser, proctologist, or anal-retentive hearing specialist, they've got to be sitting on the front step when the door opens. Heaven forbid waiting until mid-morning or early afternoon to avoid rush-hour traffic. Hell no, they have to get out there and congest the highways, see how many people they can make late for work, maybe even throw in a fender-bender or two.

Unfortunately, morning satisfaction is not enough for some of these oldsters. About four in the afternoon, they hit the road again to wreak havoc on the poor folks getting off work. Lord knows, they can't afford to miss that early-bird senior discount at the all-you-can-eat buffet. Why, if they can make it back home by six-thirty, they might even catch the first half of "Wheel of Fortune" before falling asleep in the recliner.

I guess I shouldn't complain. Someday I'll be old too – if I live long enough. Just think of all the employment opportunities these old people generate for traffic cops, insurance adjusters, and paramedics. They certainly do their part to stimulate the economy.

But for safety's sake, isn't it about time we labeled their automobiles? A simple solution would be to plaster "OLD DRIVER" across the back of their Cadillac or Lincoln Towncar. If you prefer a kinder, gentler expression of geriatric notation, I propose "BLUE-HAIR BEHIND THE WHEEL," or the gender friendly "OCTOGENARIAN OPERATOR."

Now, some of you may think it cruel and demeaning to label our senior's vehicles. Get over it. If the federal government can mandate seatbelts, child restraints, and McDonalds coffee temperature in the name of public safety, then why not flag the old geezer's starship?

Like I tell my grandson, "If you don't like the way I drive . . . stay off the sidewalk."

Acknowledgements

This book comes with no guarantees. If you're not completely satisfied, here's a list of individuals you can blame. Each of them contributed to this book in some form or fashion.

- ☺ God, for giving me a sense of humor and creating an opportunity for me to use it.
- ☺ Linda C. Apple, who introduced me to the Northwest Arkansas Writers' Workshop.
- ☺ All my brothers and sisters at the critique group and especially our matriarch and patriarch, Velda Brotherton and Dusty Richards.
- ☺ JB Hogan and Martha Estes, who encourage and support ridiculous behavior at every available opportunity.
- ☺ Duke and Kimberly Pennell, who risked their reputation as serious publishers by promoting this collection of shorts.
- ☺ And most importantly, my loving wife, Connie Gayer, who has stood by me and supported me in all my endeavors.

About the Author

 Like Benjamin Franklin, Russell Gayer spent most of his adult life in the printing industry, except for three years in which he was a framing carpenter, honing skills that his wife, Connie, has made sure come in handy ever since. Unlike Franklin, he has not made any major discoveries (other than Home Project Shock Syndrome), invented anything significant, or made lasting contributions for the betterment of his fellow man. Until this book, that is.

Find more of his humor at RussellGayer.com.

If you like this book enough to review it and think others would enjoy it too, please post at Amazon.com and/or Pen-L.com.

Thanks!

Made in the USA
San Bernardino, CA
26 April 2014